little aran & celtic
knits for kids

little aran & celtic knits for kids

25 designs for babies and young children

Martin Storey

photography by Steven Wooster

St Martins Griffin
New York

Little Aran & Celtic Knits for Kids

Copyright © 2013 by Berry & Bridges Ltd.

All rights reserved. Printed in China.
For information, address St. Martin's Press,
175 Fifth Avenue, New York, N.Y. 10010.

www.stmartins.com

Library of Congress Cataloging-in-Publication
Data Available Upon Request

ISBN 978-1-250-03907-1

First U.S. Edition: October 2013

10 9 8 7 6 5 4 3 2 1

Designer Anne Wilson
Editor Katie Hardwicke
Styling Susan Berry
Pattern writing and knitting Penny Hill
Pattern checker Marilyn Wilson
Charts Therese Chynoweth
Illustrations Ed Berry

Contents

heidi coat

A sweet, slightly flared, double-breasted coat or jacket, Heidi has a lovely textured design and really great shape. It is perfect for layering over a skirt, dress, or leggings. Knitted in Rowan *Wool Cotton 4 Ply* (see pattern, page 50).

tobias hoodie

This great Aran cabled hoodie would suit both boys and girls. It has a generous hood that extends from a shawl collar neckline. The sleeves and back are worked in plain seed stitch. Knitted in Rowan *Wool Cotton* (see pattern, page 54).

petra sweater

This lovely little sweater with its charming cat, mouse, and leaf motifs, is sure to appeal to young children. The hem and cuffs are tipped in green, echoing the green leaves. A buttoned shoulder fastening makes it easy to put on and take off. Knitted in *Rowan Fine Tweed* (see pattern, page 58).

jakob cardigan

This time a button-up collared cardigan for boys features hares and foxes running around the front and back, and around the sleeves. Knitted in *Rowan Fine Tweed* (see pattern, page 62).

stefan sweater

This little boy's sweater uses one of the Scandinavian seafaring patterns in the form of an anchor in the center front panel. It has a slighter lowered crew neck and a buttoned shoulder fastening. Knitted in Rowan *Wool Cotton 4 Ply* (see pattern, page 68).

lotte cardigan

These characterful little birds, interspersed with rows of simple Fairisle, make a delightful buttoned up, collared, cropped cardigan for little girls. Knitted in *Rowan Fine Tweed* (see pattern, page 72).

lotte scarf

The little bird motif (see also the Lotte cardigan) makes a great addition to a narrow scarf, knitted double, tipped with one of the colors from the bird, and with a little repeating Fairisle pattern. (The scarecrow, made by Noa who is lying next to it, looks pretty good in it too!) Knitted in *Rowan Fine Tweed* (see pattern, page 78).

sofie tunic

This sweet little tunic, with its lightly gathered skirt, sports a heart motif on the front panel. The neck is a lowered round neck, worked in seed stitch to give it a flat edge, as is the hem. Knitted in Rowan *Wool Cotton 4 Ply* (see pattern, page 80).

olle socks & mittens

Stripes are always fun to knit and a useful way of using up your "stash" of yarns from other colorwork patterns. If you don't have quite enough of any one color, you can bring in the changes on the stripe sequence to suit. Knitted in Rowan *Felted Tweed DK* (see Socks pattern, page 84, and Mittens pattern, page 86).

alexa poncho

With its heavily cabled and bobbled front and twisted cable hem, this little poncho with a generous hood, makes a great winter cover-up but is light enough to wear as a loose sweater, too. Knitted in Rowan *Wool Cotton* (see pattern, page 88).

josef vest

This little button-through vest with a neat shawl collar, has a great checkerboard texture pattern, which is fun to knit. Knitted in Rowan *Wool Cotton 4 Ply* (see pattern, page 92).

alphabet throw & blocks

Two more great projects that you can work on the go, as the pieces are joined later. The letters on the throw are interspersed with other simple motifs. You can use the whole alphabet, as here, or create a child's name or a simple message if you prefer. Knitted in Rowan *Felted Tweed DK* (see Throw pattern, page 96, and Blocks pattern, page 102).

morten jacket

This classic cable design with its shawl collar, makes a warm winter cover-up for a little boy. Knitted in *Rowan Fine Tweed*, it is cozy and comfortable to wear (see pattern, page 104).

mikal slipover

This textured slipover with a split front neck, would look equally good on a little girl, perhaps in a lighter colorway. Knitted in Rowan *Wool Cotton* (see pattern, page 109).

aneka cardigan

A great classic Aran design in miniature, this makes a lovely warm cardigan for a little girl and provides the knitter with lots of interest. Knitted in Rowan *Siena 4 Ply* (see pattern, page 112).

bo cardigan

This long length cardigan is a must for all lovers of colorwork who want to make something really special for a little girl, or boy. Its brilliant "houses" motif is worked across the fronts and the back, above a repeating border of different hearts, which also features on the sleeves. Knitted in *Rowan Fine Tweed* (see pattern, page 116).

folk scarf & bag

This great folk people motif features both on the pockets at each end of the striped scarf and on the matching tiny tote bag. Knitted in Rowan *Felted Tweed DK* (see Bag pattern, page 122, and Scarf pattern, page 125).

norse hat & scarf

Knitted in Rowan *Felted Tweed DK*, this simple two-tone stripe and bird's-eye Fairisle combination, with its two by two rib in a contrasting color, is lovely to knit. It would work well for both boys and girls. (See Scarf pattern, page 127, and Hat pattern, page 129).

lara sweater

The pattern of this charming textured sweater shows up beautifully in Rowan *Cotton Glacé*. It has a split buttoned neck to make it easy to get on and off. (See pattern, page 130.)

finn sweater

A lovely, very simple fine-cable classic sweater with a small roll neck, it has a very stretchy shape and can be worn by both boys and girls. Knitted in Rowan *Wool Cotton* (see pattern, page 134).

tundra cushion

This wonderful colorwork pattern is both classic and contemporary, and gives a touch of class to any nursery. It has a simple striped back. Knitted in Rowan *Felted Tweed DK* (see pattern, page 137).

the patterns

heidi coat

A lovely little double-breasted short coat with an A-line shape, Heidi has lots of cable and texture detail to add interest to the design. It looks equally good worn with a skirt or dress, or leggings. Rowan *Wool Cotton 4 Ply* shows up the stitch pattern beautifully but is also soft and comfortable to wear.

Sizes

To fit ages

6–9	12–18	24–36	36–48	months

Actual measurements

Chest

20¾	22½	24¾	27½	in
53	57	63	70	cm

Length to shoulder

13½	15	17	19¼	in
34	38	43	49	cm

Sleeve length

6¾	8¼	9¾	11½	in
17	21	25	29	cm

Yarn

6(6:7:7) x 1¾oz/197yd balls of Rowan *Wool Cotton 4 Ply* Leaf 491

Needles

Pair each of size 2/3 (3mm) and size 3 (3.25mm) knitting needles
Cable needle

Extras

Stitch holders
Six buttons

Gauge

28 sts and 36 rows to 4in/10cm square over rev St st using size 3 (3.25mm) needles.
36 sts and 38 rows to 4in/10cm square over cable patt using size 3 (3.25mm) needles.
Or size to obtain correct gauge.

Abbreviations

K1tbl = knit through the back of the loop.
P1tbl = purl through the back of the loop.
C4B = slip next 2 sts onto a cable needle and hold at back of work, k2, then k2 from cable needle.
C4F = slip next 2 sts onto a cable needle and hold at front of work, k2, then k2 from cable needle.
Cr2R = slip next st onto cable needle and hold at back of work, k1tbl, then p1 from cable needle.
Cr2L = slip next st onto cable needle and hold at front of work, p1, then k1tbl from cable needle.
See also page 141.

Note

When working from Chart, right side rows read from right to left and wrong side rows from left to right.

Back

Using size 3 (3.25mm) needles, cast on 102(124:146:168) sts.
Row 1 (RS) P4(5:6:7), [work across row 1 of panel A, p2(4:6:8), work across row 1 of panel B, p2(4:6:8)] 5 times, work across row 1 of panel A, p4(5:6:7).
Row 2 K4(5:6:7), [work across row 2 of panel A, k2(4:6:8), work across row 2 of panel B, k2(4:6:8)] 5 times, work across row 2 of panel A, k4(5:6:7).
These 2 rows set the panels with rev St st at sides.
Work even until back measures 6¼(7:8¼:9¾)in/ 16(18:21:25)cm from cast-on edge, ending with a wrong side row.
Dec row P4(5:6:7), * patt panel A, [p2tog] 1(2:3:4) time(s), patt panel B, [p2tog] 1(2:3:4) time(s); rep from * 4 times, then patt panel A, p4(5:6:7).
92(104:116:128) sts.
Work a further 2(2¼:2¾:3¼)in/5(6:7:8)cm, ending with a wrong side row.
Shape armholes
Bind off 3(4:5:6) sts at beg of next 2 rows.
86(96:106:116) sts.
Work even until back measures 13½(15:17:19¼)in/ 34(38:43:49)cm from cast-on edge, ending with a wrong side row.
Shape shoulders
Bind off 10(12:14:16) sts at beg of next 4 rows.
Bind off rem 46(48:50:52) sts.

Left front

Using size 3 (3.25mm) needles, cast on 40(49:58:67) sts.
Row 1 (RS) P4(5:6:7), [work across row 1 of panel A, p2(4:6:8), work across row 1 of panel B, p2(4:6:8)] twice, p2.
Row 2 K2, [k2(4:6:8), work across row 2 of panel B, k2(4:6:8), work across row 2 of panel A] twice, k4(5:6:7).
These 2 rows set the panels with rev St st at side.
Work even until front measures 6¼(7:8¼:9¾)in/ 16(18:21:25)cm from cast-on edge, ending with a wrong side row.

Panel A

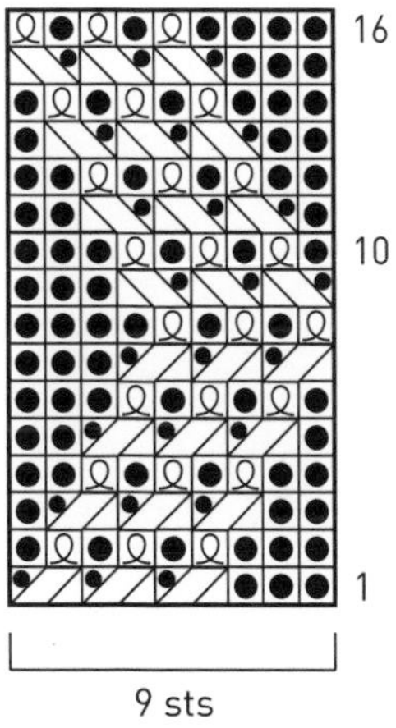
16
10
1
9 sts

Panel B

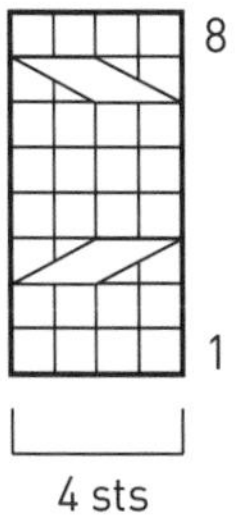
8
1
4 sts

Key

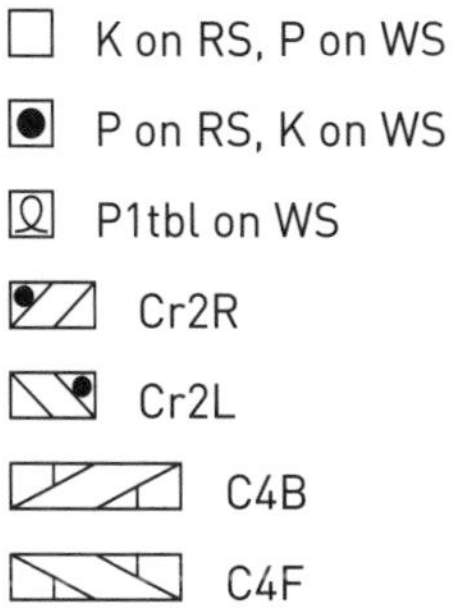
K on RS, P on WS
P on RS, K on WS
P1tbl on WS
Cr2R
Cr2L
C4B
C4F

Dec row P4(5:6:7), * patt panel A, [p2tog] 1(2:3:4) time(s), patt panel B, [p2tog] 1(2:3:4) time(s); rep from * once, p2. *36(41:46:51) sts.*

Work a further 2(2¼:2¾:3¼)in/5(6:7:8)cm, ending with a wrong side row.

Shape armhole

Next row Bind off 3(4:5:6) sts, patt. 33(37:41:45) sts. Work even until front measures 11½(13:14½:17)in/ 29(33:37:43)cm from cast-on edge, ending with a wrong side row.

Shape front neck

Next row Patt to last 2 sts, work 2tog.

Next row Work 2tog, patt to end.

Rep the last 2 rows until 20(24:28:32) sts rem. Work even until front measures the same as back to shoulder, ending at armhole edge.

Shape shoulder

Next row Bind off 10(12:14:16) sts, patt to end.

Work 1 row.

Bind off rem sts.

Right front

Using size 3 (3.25mm) needles, cast on 40(49:58:67) sts.

Row 1 (RS) P2, [p2(4:6:8), work across row 1 of panel B, p2(4:6:8), work across row 1 of panel A] twice, p4(5:6:7).

Row 2 K4(5:6:7), [work across row 2 of panel A, k2(4:6:8), work across row 2 of panel B, k2(4:6:8)] twice, k2.

These 2 rows set the panels with rev St st at sides. Work even until front measures 6¼(7:8¼:9¾)in/ 16(18:21:25)cm from cast-on edge, ending with a wrong side row.

Dec row P2, * [p2tog] 1(2:3:4) time(s), patt panel B, [p2tog] 1(2:3:4) time(s), patt panel A; rep from * once more, p4(5:6:7). *36(41:46:51) sts.*

Work a further 2(2¼:2¾:3¼)in/5(6:7:8)cm, ending with a right side row.

Shape armhole

Next row Bind off 3(4:5:6) sts, patt. 33(37:41:45) sts.

Work even until front measures 11½(13:14½:17)in/ 29(33:37:43)cm in from cast-on edge, ending with a wrong side row.

Shape front neck

Next row Work 2tog, patt to end.

Next row Patt to last 2 sts, work 2tog.

Rep the last 2 rows until 20(24:28:32) sts rem. Work even until front measures the same as back to shoulder, ending at armhole edge.

Shape shoulder

Next row Bind off 10(12:14:16) sts, patt to end.

Work 1 row.

Bind off rem sts.

Sleeves

Using size 3 (3.25mm) needles, cast on 59(63:69:73) sts.

Row 1 (RS) P4(4:5:5), [work across row 1 of panel A, p4(5:6:7), work across row 1 of panel B, p4(5:6:7)] twice, work across row 1 of panel A, p4(4:5:5).

Row 2 K4(4:5:5), [work across row 2 of panel A, k4(5:6:7), work across row 2 of panel B, k4(4:6:7)] twice, work across row 2 of panel A, k4(4:5:5).

These 2 rows set the panels with rev St st at sides. Work a further 2 rows.

Inc row P2, m1, patt to last 2 sts, m1, p2.

Work 5(7:9:11) rows.

Rep the last 6(8:10:12) rows 7 times more and the inc row again, working all inc sts into rev St st. *77(81:87:91) sts.*

Work even until sleeve measures 6¾(8¼:9¾:11½)in/ 17(21:25:29)cm from cast-on edge, ending with a wrong side row.

Mark each end of last row with a colored thread.

Work 2(4:6:8) rows.

Bind off.

Buttonband

Using size 3 (3.25mm) needles, cast on 39(43:47:51) sts.

Row 1 (RS) P1, [k1tbl, p1] to end.

Row 2 P1, [p1tbl, k1] to end.

These 2 rows form the twisted rib with one garter-st edge st.

Cont in rib until band fits up left front edge.

Leave these sts on a holder.

Mark position for 6 buttons, the first pair 1¼in/3cm from neck edge, the third pair level with dec row on front, and the remaining pair halfway between.

Buttonhole band

Using size 3 (3.25mm) needles, cast on 39(43:47:51) sts.

Row 1 (RS) P1, [k1tbl, p1] to end.

Row 2 K1, [p1tbl, k1] to last 2 sts, p1tbl, p1.

These 2 rows form the twisted rib with one garter-st edge st.

Cont in rib until band fits up right front edge, working buttonholes to match markers as foll:

Buttonhole row (RS) Rib 4, k2tog, y2o, skpo, rib to last 8 sts, k2tog, y2o, skpo, rib 4.

Leave these sts on a holder.

Collar

Join shoulder seams.

With right side facing, using size 2/3 (3mm) needles, rib 37(41:45:49) sts from buttonhole band, work 2tog, pick up and k18(18:20:20) sts up right front neck edge, 45(47:49:51) from back neck, pick up and k18(18:20:20) down left side of front neck, work 2tog, rib 37(41:45:49) from buttonband. *157(167:181:191) sts.*

Cont in rib as set.

Rows 1 and 2 Rib to last 56(60:66:70) sts, turn.

Rows 3 and 4 Rib to last 53(57:62:66) sts, turn.

Rows 5 and 6 Rib to last 50(54:58:62) sts, turn.

Rows 7 and 8 Rib to last 46(50:54:58) sts, turn.

Rows 9 and 10 Rib to last 42(46:50:54) sts, turn.

Rows 11 and 12 Rib to last 38(42:46:50) sts, turn.

Change to size 3 (3.25mm) needles.

Reverse the rib from now by working k1tbl over p1 sts and p1 over k1tbl, to form fold line.

Rows 13 and 14 Rib to last 32(36:40:44) sts, turn.

Rows 15 and 16 Rib to last 26(30:34:38) sts, turn.

Rows 17 and 18 Rib to last 20(24:28:32) sts, turn.

Rows 19 and 20 Rib to last 14(18:22:26) sts, turn.

Rows 21 and 22 Rib to last 8(12:16:20) sts, turn.

Rows 23 and 24 Rib to last 4(8:10:14) sts, turn.

2nd, 3rd, and 4th sizes only

Rows 25 and 26 Rib to last -(4:4:8) sts, turn.

4th size only

Rows 27 and 28 Rib to last -(-:-:4) sts, turn.

All sizes

Rib to end.

Bind off in rib.

Finishing

Sew front bands in place. Join side and sleeve seams to colored threads. Sew in sleeves. Sew on buttons.

tobias hoodie

A modern take on a traditional Aran design, this generously hooded sweater in Rowan *Wool Cotton* will have equal appeal for boys and girls. The cabled panel at the front is complimented by a plain seed stitch back and sleeves.

Sizes

To fit ages

6–9	12–18	24–36	36–48	months

Actual measurements

Chest

21¼	22¾	24½	25½	in
54	58	62	65	cm

Length to shoulder

10¾	11¾	13½	15¼	in
27	30	34	39	cm

Sleeve length

6¾	8¼	9¾	11½	in
17	21	25	29	cm

Yarn

6(7:7:8) x 1¾oz/123yd balls of Rowan *Wool Cotton* Antique 900

Needles

Pair each of size 5 (3.75mm) and size 6 (4mm) knitting needles
Size 5 (3.75mm) circular needle
Cable needle

Gauge

22 sts and 30 rows to 4in/10cm square over St st using size 6 (4mm) needles.
22 sts and 36 rows to 4in/10cm square over seed st using size 6 (4mm) needles.
Or size to obtain correct gauge.

Abbreviations

K1tbl = knit through the back of the loop.
P1tbl = purl through the back of the loop.
C4B = slip next 2 sts onto cable needle and hold at back of work, k2, then k2 from cable needle.
C4F = slip next 2 sts onto cable needle and hold at front of work, k2, then k2 from cable needle.
C4R = slip next 2 sts onto cable needle and hold at back of work, k2, then p2 from cable needle.
C4L = slip next 2 sts onto cable needle and hold at front of work, p2, then k2 from cable needle.
T4R = slip next st onto cable needle and hold at back of work, k1tbl, p1, k1tbl, then p1 from cable needle.
T4L = slip next 3 sts onto cable needle and hold at front of work, p1, then k1tbl, p1, k1tbl, from cable needle.
T7B = slip next 4 sts onto cable needle and hold at back of work, k1tbl, p1, k1tbl, then [p1, k1tbl] twice, from cable needle.
See also page 141.

Note

When working from Chart, right side rows are read from right to left and wrong side rows from left to right.

Back

Using size 5 (3.75mm) needles, cast on 62(66:70:74) sts.
Rib row (RS) [K1, p1] to end.
Rep this row 5(7:9:11) times more.
Change to size 6 (4mm) needles.
Seed st row 1 [K1, p1] to end.
Seed st row 2 [P1, k1] to end.
These 2 rows form the seed st.
Cont in seed st until back measures 5½(6¼:7½:9)in/14(16:19:23)cm from cast-on edge, ending with a wrong side row.

Shape armholes

Bind off 4 sts at beg of next 2
rows. *54(58:62:66) sts.*
Work even until back
measures 10¾(11¾:13½:15¼)
in/27(30:34:39)cm from cast-on
edge, ending with a wrong side
row.

Shape shoulders

Bind off 6(7:8:9) sts at beg of next
2 rows and 7(8:9:10) sts at beg of
foll 2 rows.
Bind off rem 28(28:28:28) sts.

Front

Using size 5 (3.75mm) needles,
cast on 62(66:70:74) sts.
Rib row (RS) [K1, p1] to end.
Rep this row 4(6:8:10) times
more.
Inc row Rib 10(12:14:16), m1, [rib
6, m1] 7 times, rib 10(12:14:16).
70(74:78:82) sts.
Change to size 6 (4mm) needles.
Row 1 [K1, p1] 5(6:7:8) times, p2,
work across row 1 of Charts A, B,
A, p2, [k1, p1] 5(6:7:8) times.
Row 2 [P1, k1] 5(6:7:8) times, k2,
work across row 2 of Charts A, B,
A, k2, [p1, k1] 5(6:7:8) times.
These 2 rows set the cable
panels with seed st at sides.
Cont in patt until front measures
5½(6¼:7½:9)in/14(16:19:23)cm
from cast-on edge, ending with a
wrong side row.

Shape armholes

Bind off 4 sts at beg of next 2
rows. *62(66:70:74) sts.*
Work 6 rows.

Chart A

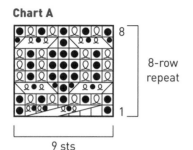

8-row
repeat

9 sts

Chart B

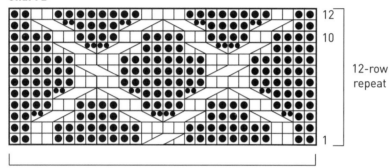

12

10

12-row
repeat

1

28 sts

Key

☐	K on RS, P on WS
●	P on RS, K on WS
Ⓠ	K1tbl on RS, P1tbl on WS
▱	C4B
▱	C4F
▱	C4R
▱	C4L
▱	T4R
▱	T4L
▱	T7B

Divide for neck

Row 1 Patt 19(21:23:25), turn and work on these sts.

Work 3 rows.

Dec row Patt to last 14 sts, p2tog, patt to end.

Work 7 rows.

Rep the last 8 rows twice more and the dec row again. *15(17:19:21) sts.*

Work even until front measures the same as back to shoulder, ending at armhole edge.

Shape shoulder

Next row Bind off 6(7:8:9) sts, patt to end.

Work 1 row.

Bind off rem sts.

With right side facing, rejoin yarn to rem sts, bind off center 24 sts, patt to end. *19(21:23:25) sts.*

Work 3 rows.

Dec row Patt 12, p2tog, patt to end.

Work 7 rows.

Rep the last 8 rows twice more and the dec row again. *15(17:19:21) sts.*

Work even until front measures the same as back to shoulder, ending at armhole edge.

Shape shoulder

Next row Bind off 6(7:8:9) sts, patt to end.

Work 1 row.

Bind off rem sts.

Sleeves

Using size 5 (3.75mm) needles, cast on 34(36:38:40) sts.

Rib row (RS) [K1, p1] to end.

Rep this row 5(7:9:11) times more.

Change to size 6 (4mm) needles.

Seed st row 1 [K1, p1] to end.

Seed st row 2 [P1, k1] to end.

These 2 rows form the seed st.

Inc and work into seed st, one st at each end of the next

and every foll 4th row. *54(60:66:70) sts.*
Work even until sleeve measures 6¾(8¼:9¾:11½)in/
17(21:25:29)cm from cast-on edge, ending with a
wrong side row.
Mark each end of last row with a colored thread.
Work a further 6 rows.
Bind off.

Hood

Using size 6 (4mm) needles, cast on 42 sts.
Seed st row 1 [K1, p1] to end.
Seed st row 2 [P1, k1] to end.
These 2 rows form the seed st.
Cont in seed st until work measures 8¾(9:9½:9¾)in/
22(23:24:25)cm from cast-on edge, ending with a
wrong side row.
Shape top
Next row Patt 21, turn and work on these sts.
Next row Bind off 5 sts, patt to end.
Next row Patt to end.
Rep the last 2 rows twice more.
Bind off rem 6 sts.
With right side facing, rejoin yarn to rem sts.
Next row Bind off 5 sts, patt to end.
Next row Patt to end.
Rep the last 2 rows twice more.
Bind off rem sts.

Edging

Join shoulder seams. Sew cast-on edge of hood to
neck edge.
With right side facing, using size 5 (3.75mm) circular
needle, pick up and k30(32:34:36) sts up right side
of front neck, 66(68:70:72) sts up right side of hood,
66(68:70:72) sts down left side of hood, 30(32:34:36) sts
down left side of front neck. *192(200:208:216) sts.*
1st row P3, [k2, p2] to last 5 sts, k2, p3.
2nd row K3, [p2, k2] to last 5 sts, p2, k3.
Rep the last 2 rows 17 times more.
Bind off in rib.

Finishing

Sew in sleeves with last 6 rows to 4 sts bind off at
underarm. Join side and sleeve seams. Lap left side of
hood ribbing over right and stitch in place.

petra sweater

A cute colorwork sweater that will appeal to both boys and girls, Petra is knitted in *Rowan Fine Tweed*, a yarn that really lends itself to working color patterns. The hem, neck, and cuffs are trimmed in contrasting colored yarn. The side buttons at the neck make getting it on and off much easier!

Sizes

To fit ages

6–9	12–18	24–36	36–48	months

Actual measurements

Chest

21¼	23¼	25	26¾	in
54	59	64	68	cm

Length to shoulder

11½	12½	14¼	16¼	in
29	32	36	41	cm

Sleeve length

6¾	8¼	9¾	11½	in
17	21	25	29	cm

Yarns

Rowan Fine Tweed

4(5:5:6) x 1oz/98yd balls Arncliffe 360 (M)

One ball each Nidd 382 (A), Settle 374 (B), Richmond 381 (C), and Hawes 362 (D)

Needles

Pair each of size 2 (2.75mm) and size 3 (3.25mm) knitting needles

Extras

Stitch holders

3 buttons

Gauge

26 sts and 36 rows to 4in/10cm square over patt on size 3 (3.25mm) needles, *or size to obtain correct gauge.*

Abbreviations

See page 141.

Note

When working from Chart, right side rows are read from right to left and wrong side rows from left to right. Use the Fairisle method and strand yarn across back of work over no more than 3 sts. For the size you are making, take off the center st from the number of sts you have left, divide the remainder by 2, and count this number either side of the center st, this will be your starting and finishing point.

Back

Using size 2 (2.75mm) needles and C, cast on 73(79:85:91) sts.

Rib row 1 K1, [p1, k1] to end.

Break off C.

Cont in M.

Rib row 2 P1, [k1, p1] to end.

Rep the last 2 rib rows 5(6:6:7) times more.

Change to size 3 (3.25mm) needles.

Work in St st and patt from Chart.

When chart is completed, cont in M only until back measures 11(12¼:13¾:15¾)in/28(31:35:40)cm from cast-on edge, ending with a purl row.

Shape upper arms

Bind off 4 sts at beg of next 2 rows and 4(5:6:7) sts at beg of foll 2 rows. *57(61:65:69) sts.*

Bind off 14(15:16:17) sts, knit to last 14(15:16:17) sts, p0(1:0:1), [k1, p1] 7(7:8:8) times, turn and work in rib on these 14(15:16:17) sts.

Work a further 6 rows.

Bind off in rib.

Leave rem 29(31:33:35) sts on a holder.

Front

Work as given for back until front measures 9½(10¼:11¾:13½)in/24(26:30:34)cm from cast-on edge, ending with a wrong side row.

Shape front neck

Next row K27(29:31:33) sts, turn and work on these sts for first side of neck shaping.

Dec one st at neck edge on the next 5 rows. *22(24:26:28) sts.*

Work even until 4 rows less have been worked than on back to upper arm shaping, ending with a purl row.

Next row K8(9:10:11), [p1, k1] 7(7:8:8) times, p0(1:0:1).

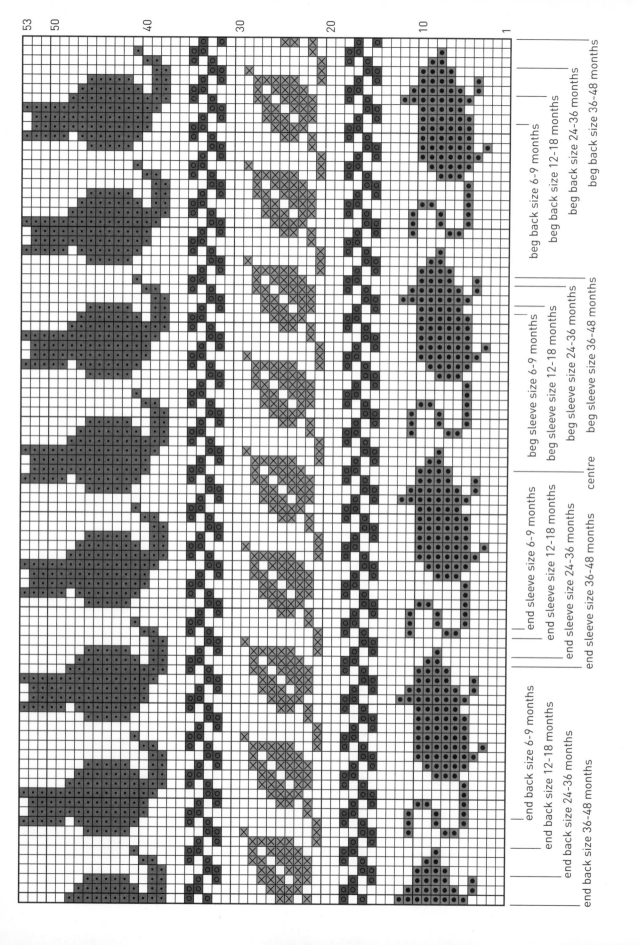

Key

☐ Arncliffe (M) ▦ Settle (B) ◉ Hawes (D)

● Nidd (A) ⊠ Richmond (C)

Next row Rib 14(15:16:17), p8(9:10:11).

Buttonhole row K8(9:10:11), rib 3, yo, k2tog, rib 5, yo, p2tog, rib to end.

Work 1 row.

Shape upper arm

Bind off 4 sts at beg of next row and 4(5:6:7) sts at beg of foll right side row.

Bind off in rib.

With right side facing, slip center 19(21:23:25) sts on a holder, rejoin yarn to rem sts, knit to end.

Dec one st at neck edge on the next 5 rows.

22(24:26:28) sts.

Work even until front measures the same as upper arm shaping, ending at side edge.

Shape upper arm

Bind off 4 sts at beg of next row and 4(5:6:7) sts at beg of foll wrong side row.

Work 1 row.

Bind off.

Sleeves

Using size 2 (2.75mm) needles and C, cast on 32(34:38:40) sts.

Next row [K1, p1] to end.

This row forms the rib.

Break off C.

Join on M.

The last row forms the rib.

Work 11(13:13:15) more rows, inc one st at end of last row. *33(35:39:41) sts.*

Change to size 3 (3.25mm) needles. Work in St st and patt from Chart.

Inc and work into patt one st at each end of the 5th and every foll 4th row until there are 57(61:65:71) sts.

Cont straight until sleeve measures 6¾(8¼:9¾:11½)in/ 17(21:25:29)cm from cast-on edge, ending with a wrong side row.

Bind off.

Neckband

Join right shoulder seam.

With right side facing, using size 2 (2.75mm) needles and M, pick up and k15(17:17:19) sts down left side of front neck, k19(21:23:25) sts from front neck holder, pick up and k15(17:17:19) sts up right side of front neck, k29(31:33:35) sts from back neck holder, pick up and k7 sts along row ends of buttonband.

85(93:97:105) sts.

Rib row 1 K1, [p1, k1] to end.

Rib row 2 P1, [k1, p1] to end.

Buttonhole row Rib to last 5 sts, yo, p2tog, rib 3.

Rib 2 more rows.

Break off M.

Join on B.

Rib 2 more rows.

Bind off in rib.

Finishing

Lap buttonhole band over buttonband and stitch in place. Sew on sleeves. Join side and sleeve seams. Sew on buttons.

jakob cardigan

A cardigan this time, with another lovely colorwork design, also knitted in *Rowan Fine Tweed*. In Jakob, the pattern goes around the sleeves as well as across the fronts and back.

Sizes

To fit ages

6–9	12–18	24–36	36–48	months

Actual measurements

Chest

21¼	22¾	24½	26	in
54	58	62	66	cm

Length to shoulder

11½	12½	14¼	16¼	in
29	32	36	41	cm

Sleeve length

6¾	8¼	9¾	11½	in
17	21	25	29	cm

Yarns

Rowan Fine Tweed

5(5:6:6) x 1oz/98yd balls Nappa 380 (M)

One ball each Pendle 377 (A), Malham 366 (B), Hubberholme 370 (C), and Dent 373 (D)

Needles

Pair each of size 2 (2.75mm) and size 3 (3.25mm) knitting needles

Extras

Stitch holders

5(5:6:6) buttons

Gauge

26 sts and 36 rows to 4in/10cm square over patt on size 3 (3.25mm) needles, *or size to obtain correct gauge*.

Abbreviations

See page 141.

Note

When working from Charts, right side rows are read from right to left and wrong side rows from left to right.

Back

Using size 2 (2.75mm) needles and M, cast on 73(79:85:91) sts.

Rib row 1 K1, [p1, k1] to end.

Rib row 2 P1, [k1, p1] to end.

Rep the last 2 rows 5(6:6:7) times more.

Change to size 3 (3.25mm) needles.

Work in St st and patt from Charts.

Row 1 Using M, knit to end.

Row 2 Using M, purl to end.

Row 3 K3(5:7:9)M, [knit across 21 sts of row 1 of rabbit motif, k2(3:4:5)M] twice, work across row 1 of rabbit motif, k3(5:7:9)M.

Row 4 P3(5:7:9)M, [purl across 21 sts of row 2 of rabbit motif, p2(3:4:5)M] twice, work across row 2 of rabbit motif, p3(5:7:9)M.

These 2 rows set the patt.

Work a further 13 rows to complete motif.

Rows 18 and 19 Work 2 rows M.

Row 20 Using B, purl to end.

Row 21 K1B, [5M, 1B] to end.

Row 22 P1B, [1M, 3B, 1M, 1B] to end.

Row 23 As row 21.

Row 24 As row 20.

Rows 25 and 26 Work 2 rows M.

Row 27 K2(3:4:5)M, [knit across 14 sts of row 1 of leaf motif, k0(1:2:3)M] 4 time(s), work across row 1 of leaf motif, k1(2:3:4)M.

Row 28 P1(2:3:4)M, [purl across 14 sts of row 2 of leaf motif, p0(1:2:3)M] 4 time(s), work across row 2 of leaf motif, p2(3:4:5)M.

These 2 rows set the patt.

Work a further 7 rows to complete motif.

Rows 36–44 As rows 18–26.

Row 45 K8(9:4:4)M, [knit across 18 sts of row 1 of fox motif, k2(4:2:4)M] 2(2:3:3) times, work across row 1 of fox motif, k7(8:3:3)M.

Row 46 P7(8:3:3)M, [purl across 18 sts of row 2 of fox motif, p2(4:2:4)M] 2(2:3:3) times, work across row 2 of fox motif, p8(9:4:4)M.

Fox Motif

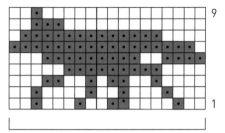

18-st repeat

Leaf Motif

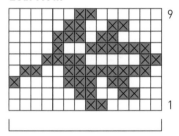

14-st repeat

Rabbit Motif

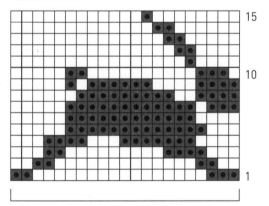

21-st repeat

Key

☐ Nappa (M)

▦ Pendle (A)

☒ Hubberholme (C)

▦ Dent (D)

These 2 rows set the patt.

Work a further 7 rows to complete motif.

Rows 54–60 As rows 18–24.

1st and 2nd sizes only

Work rows 1–24 again.

3rd and 4th sizes only

Work rows 1–42 again.

All sizes

Cont in M only until back measures 11(12¼:13¾:15¾) in/28(31:35:40)cm from cast-on edge, ending with a purl row.

Shape upper arms

Bind off 4 sts at beg of next 2 rows and 4(5:6:7) sts at beg of foll 2 rows. *57(61:65:69) sts.*

Bind off 7(7:8:8) sts at beg of next 2 rows and 7(8:8:9) sts at beg of foll 2 rows.

Bind off rem 29(31:33:35) sts.

Left front

Using size 2 (2.75mm) needles and M, cast on 41(43:47:49) sts.

Rib row 1 P1, [k1, p1] to last 2 sts, k2.

Rib row 2 K1, [p1, k1] to end.

Rep the last 2 rows twice more.

Buttonhole row Rib to last 8 sts, p2tog, y2o, k2tog, rib 4.

Work a further 4(6:6:8) rows.

Next row Rib 11, leave these sts on a holder, cast on one st, rib to end, inc 1(2:1:2) st(s) evenly. *32(35:38:41) sts.*

Change to size 3 (3.25mm) needles.

Work in St st and patt from Charts.

Row 1 Using M, knit to end.

Row 2 Using M, purl to end.

Row 3 K3(5:7:9)M, knit across 21 sts of row 1 of rabbit motif, k2(3:4:5)M, knit across first 6 sts of row 1 of rabbit motif.

Row 4 Purl across last 6 sts of row 2 of rabbit motif, p2(3:4:5)M, work across row 2 of rabbit motif, p3(5:7:9)M. Work a further 13 rows to complete motif.

Rows 18 and 19 Work 2 rows M.

Row 20 Using B, purl to end.

Row 21 K1B, [5M, 1B] to last 1(4:1:4) st(s), 1(4:1:4)M.

Row 22 P0(3:0:3)B, 0(1:0:1)M, 2(1:2:1)B, [1M, 3B, 1M, 1B] to end.

Row 23 As row 21.

Row 24 As row 20.

Rows 25 and 26 Work 2 rows M.

Row 27 K2(3:4:5)M, knit across 14 sts of row 1 of leaf motif, k0(1:2:3)M across row 1 of leaf motif, k2(3:4:5)M.

Row 28 P2(3:4:5)M, purl across 14 sts of row 2 of leaf motif, p0(1:2:3)M, purl across row 2 of leaf motif, p2(3:4:5)M.

These 2 rows set the patt.

Work a further 7 rows to complete motif.

Rows 36–44 As rows 18–26.

Row 45 K3(5:7:9)M, knit across 18 sts of row 1 of fox motif, k2(3:4:5), knit across first 9 sts of row 1 of fox motif.

Row 46 Purl across last 9 sts of row 2 of fox motif, p2(3:4:5)M, purl across row 2 of fox motif, p3(5:7:9)M.

These 2 rows set the patt.

Work a further 7 rows to complete motif.

Rows 54–60 As rows 18–24.

These 60 rows set the patt.

Work rows 1–24(24:42:42) again and then cont in M only, **at the same time** when front measures 9½(10¼:11¾:13½)in/24(26:30:34)cm from cast-on edge, ending with a wrong side row.

Shape front neck

Next row Patt to last 5(6:7:8) sts, turn and leave these sts on a holder.

Dec one st at neck edge on every right side row until 22(24:26:28) sts rem.

Work even until front measures the same as back to upper arm shaping, ending at side edge.

Shape upper arm

Bind off 4 sts at beg of next row and 4(5:6:7) sts at beg of foll right side row. *14(15:16:17) sts.*

Work 1 row.

Shape shoulder

Bind off 7(7:8:8) sts at beg of next row.

Work 1 row.

Bind off rem sts.

Right front

Using size 2 (2.75mm) needles and M, cast on 41(43:47:49) sts.

Rib row 1 K2, p1, [k1, p1] to end.

Rib row 2 K1, [p1, k1] to end.

Rep the last 2 rows 4(5:5:6) times more and the first row again.

Next row Inc 1(2:1:2) st(s) evenly rib to last 11 sts, leave these sts on a holder, cast on one st. *32(35:38:41) sts.*

Change to size 3 (3.25mm) needles.

Work in St st and patt from Charts.

Row 1 Using M, knit to end.

Row 2 Using M, purl to end.

Row 3 Knit across last 6 sts of row 1 of rabbit motif, k2(3:4:5)M, knit across 21 sts of row 1 of rabbit motif, k3(5:7:9)M.

Row 4 P3(5:7:9)M, purl across row 2 of rabbit motif, p2(3:4:5)M, purl across first 6 sts of row 2 of rabbit motif.

Work a further 13 rows to complete motif.

Rows 18 and 19 Work 2 rows M.

Row 20 Using B, purl to end.

Row 21 K1(4:1:4)M, 1B, [5M, 1B] to end.

Row 22 P[1B, 1M, 3B, 1M] to last 2(5:2:5) sts, 2(1:2:1) B, 0(1:0:1)M, 0(3:0:3)B.

Row 23 As row 21.

Row 24 As row 20.

Rows 25 and 26 Work 2 rows M.

Row 27 K2(3:4:5)M, knit across 14 sts of row 1 of leaf motif, k0(1:2:3)M, knit across row 1 of leaf motif, k2(3:4:5)M.

Row 28 P2(3:4:5)M, purl across 14 sts of row 2 of leaf motif, p0(1:2:3)M, work across row 2 of leaf motif, p2(3:4:5)M.

These 2 rows set the patt.

Work a further 7 rows to complete motif.

Rows 36–44 As rows 18–26.

Row 45 Knit across last 9 sts of row 1 of fox motif, k2(3:4:5)M, knit across 18 sts of row 1 of fox motif, k3(5:7:9)M.

Row 46 P3(5:7:9)M, purl across 18 sts of row 2 of fox motif, p2(3:4:5)M, purl across first 9 sts of row 2 of fox motif.

These 2 rows set the patt.

Work a further 7 rows to complete motif.

Rows 54–60 As rows 18–24.

These 60 rows set the patt.

Work rows 1–24(24:42:42) again and then cont in M only, **at the same time** when front measures 9½(10¼:11¾:13½)in/24(26:30:34)cm from cast-on edge, ending with a wrong side row.

Shape front neck

Next row Patt 5(6:7:8) sts, leave these sts on a holder, patt to end.

Dec one st at neck edge on every right side row until 22(24:26:28) sts rem.

Work even until front measures the same as back to upper arm shaping, ending at side edge.

Shape upper arm

Bind off 4 sts at beg of next row and 4(5:6:7) sts at beg of foll wrong side row. *14(15:16:17) sts.*

Work 1 row.

Shape shoulder

Bind off 7(7:8:8) sts at beg of next row.

Work 1 row.

Bind off rem sts.

Sleeves

Using size 2 (2.75mm) needles and M, cast on 32(34:38:40) sts.

Next row [K1, p1] to end.

This row forms the rib.

Work 11(13:13:15) more rows, inc one st at end of last row. *33(35:39:41) sts.*

Change to size 3 (3.25mm) needles.

Row 1 Using M, knit to end.

Row 2 Using M, purl to end.

Row 3 K6(7:9:10)M, knit across 21 sts of row 1 of rabbit motif, k6(7:9:10)M.

Row 4 P6(7:9:10)M, purl across 21 sts of row 2 of rabbit motif, p6(7:9:10)M.

These 2 rows set the patt.

Work a further 13 rows to complete motif, at the same time, inc one st at each end of the next and 3 foll 4th rows. *41(43:47:49) sts.*

Rows 18 and 19 Work 2 rows M.

Row 20 Using B, purl to end, inc one st at each end. *43(45:49:51) sts.*

Row 21 K0(1:3:4)M, 1B, [5M, 1B] to last 0(1:3:4) st(s), k0(1:3:4)M.

Row 22 P0(0:2:3)B, 0(1:1:1)M, 1B, [1M, 3B, 1M, 1B] to last 4(5:7:4) sts, 0(1:1:1)M, 0(0:2:3)B.

Row 23 As row 21.

Row 24 As row 20. *45(47:51:53) sts.*

Rows 25 and 26 Work 2 rows M.

Row 27 K2(2:3:3)M, [knit across 14 sts of row 1 of leaf motif, k0(1:2:3)M] twice, work across row 1 of leaf motif, k1(1:2:2)M.

Row 28 P1(1:2:2)M, [purl across 14 sts of row 2 of leaf motif, p0(1:2:3)M] twice, work across row 2 of leaf motif, p2(2:3:3)M.

These 2 rows set the patt.

Work a further 7 rows to complete motif **at the same time,** inc one st at each end of next and foll 4th row. *49(51:55:57) sts.*

Rows 36 and 37 Work 2 rows M.

Row 38 Using B, purl to end, inc one st at each end. *51(53:57:59) sts.*

Row 39 K4(5:1:2)M, 1B, [5M, 1B] to last 4(5:1:2) st(s), k4(5:1:2)M.

Row 40 P0(1:0:0)M, 3(3:0:1)B, 1M, 1B, [1M, 3B, 1M, 1B] to last 4(5:1:2) st(s), 1M, 3(3:0:1)B, 0(1:0:0)M.

Row 41 As row 39.

Row 42 As row 38. *53(55:59:61) sts.*

Rows 43 and 44 Work 2 rows M.

1st and 2nd sizes only

Cont in M only, inc one st at each end of the next and 1(2) foll 4th rows. *57(61) sts.*

Cont straight until sleeve measures 17(21:-:-)cm/ 6¾(8¼:-:-)in from cast-on edge, ending with a wrong side row.

Bind off.

3rd and 4th sizes only

Row 45 K-(-:10:11)M, knit across 18 sts of row 1 of fox motif, k-(-:2:4)M, work across row 1 of fox motif, k-(-:11:10)M.

Row 46 P-(-:11:10)M, purl across 18 sts of row 2 of fox motif, p-(-:2:4)M, work across row 2 of fox motif, p-(-:10:11)M.

These 2 rows set the patt.

Work a further 7 rows to complete motif **at the same time,** inc one st at each end of next and foll 4th row. *-(-:63:65) sts.*

Cont in M only, inc one st at each end of the next and –(-:1:2) foll 4th rows. *-(-:67:71) sts.*

Cont straight until sleeve measures -(-:9¾:11½)in/ -(-:25:29)cm from cast-on edge, ending with a wrong side row.

Bind off.

Buttonband

With wrong side facing, using size 2 (2.75mm) needles and M, cast on one st, rib across sts on right front. *12 sts.*

Work in rib until band fits up right front to beg of neck shaping, ending with a right side row.

Leave these sts on a holder.

Mark position for 5(5:6:6) buttons, the first in 7th row of rib, the last 2 rows below neck shaping.

Buttonhole band

With right side facing, using size 2 (2.75mm) needles and M, cast on one st, rib across sts on left front. *12 sts.*

Work in rib until band fits up left front to beg of neck shaping, ending with a wrong side row and working buttonholes to match markers.

Buttonhole row Rib to last 4 sts, p2tog, y2o, k2tog, rib 4.

Leave these sts on a holder.

Collar

Join shoulder seams.

With right side facing, using size 2 (2.75mm) needles and M, slip sts from right front band onto a needle, then slip 5(6:7:8) sts from right front onto same holder, pick up and k16(18:20:22) sts up right side of neck, cast on 45(47:51:53) sts, pick up and k16(18:20:22) sts down left side of front neck, k5(6:7:8) sts from left front, the rib 12 sts from buttonhole band. *111(119:129:137) sts.*

Cont in rib as set.

Next 2 rows Rib to last 33(36:39:42) sts, turn.

Next 2 rows Rib to last 29(32:35:38) sts, turn.

Next 2 rows Rib to last 25(28:31:34) sts, turn.

Next 2 rows Rib to last 21(23:25:27) sts, turn.

Next 2 rows Rib to last 17(18:19:20) sts, turn.

Next 2 rows Rib to last 13(13:13:13) sts, turn.

Next row Rib to end.

Work 2 rows across all sts.

Bind off 8 sts at beg of next 2 rows.

Work a further 16(18:20:22) rows. *95(103:113:121) sts.*

Bind off in rib.

Finishing

Sew cast-on edge of collar to bound-off sts at back neck. Sew bands in place. Sew on sleeves, placing center of bound-off edge to shoulder seam. Join side and sleeve seams. Sew on buttons.

stefan sweater

A simple but effective anchor design as a front panel creates a cute Guernsey-style sweater for boys or girls. Knitted in Rowan *Wool Cotton 4 Ply*.

Sizes

To fit ages

6–9	12–18	24–36	36–48	months

Actual measurements

Chest

21½	23¼	24¾	26¾	in
55	59	63	68	cm

Length to shoulder

10½	11¾	13½	15½	in
27	30	34	39	cm

Sleeve length

6¾	8¼	9¾	11½	in
17	21	25	29	cm

Yarn

3(3:4:4) x 1¾oz/197yd balls of Rowan *Wool Cotton 4 Ply* Paper 486

Needles

Pair each of size 2 (2.75mm) and size 3 (3.25mm) knitting needles
Cable needle

Extras

Stitch holders
2 buttons

Gauge

28 sts and 36 rows to 4in/10cm square over St st on size 3 (3.25mm) needles, *or size to obtain correct gauge.*

Abbreviations

BC = slip next st onto cable needle and hold at back of work, k1, then p1 from cable needle.

FC = slip next st onto cable needle and hold at front of work, p1, then k1 from cable needle.

C2F = slip next st onto cable needle and hold at front of work, k1, then k1 from cable needle.

Cr2 = skip the first st, then purl the 2nd st, then purl the skipped st and slip both sts from the needle together.

Cr3B = slip next 2 sts onto cable needle and hold at back of work, k1, then k2 from cable needle.

Cr3F = slip next st onto cable needle and hold at front of work, k2, then k1 from cable needle.

C4B = slip next 2 sts onto cable needle and hold at back of work, k2, then k2 from cable needle.

MB = make bobble, [k1, p1, k1] all in next st, turn, p3, turn, sl 1, k2tog, psso.

See also page 141.

Note

When working from Chart, right side rows are read from right to left and wrong side rows from left to right.

Back

Using size 2 (2.75mm) needles, cast on 79(85:91:97) sts.

Rib row 1 K1, [p1, k1] to end.

Rib row 2 P1, [k1, p1] to end.

Rep the last 2 rows 5(6:6:7) times more.

Change to size 3 (3.25mm) needles.

Beg with a knit row, work in St st until back measures 6¼(7:8¼:9¾)in/16(18:21:25)cm from cast-on edge, ending with a wrong side row.

Shape armholes

Bind off 4(4:5:5) sts at beg of next 2 rows.

71(77:81:87) sts.

Next row K1, skpo, knit to last 3 sts, k2tog, k1.

Next row Purl to end.

Rep the last 2 rows 3(4:4:5) times more.

63(67:71:75) sts.

Work even until back measures 10½(11¾:13½:15¼)in/ 27(30:34:39)cm from cast-on edge, ending with a wrong side row.

Shape shoulders

Rows 1 and 2 Bind off 7(8:8:9) sts, knit to last 7(8:8:9) sts, turn, purl to end.

Row 3 Bind off 8(8:9:9) sts, knit to last 15(16:17:18) sts, [k1, p1] 7(8:8:9) times, k1(0:1:0).

Rows 4 and 5 P1(0:1:0), [k1, p1] 7(8:8:9) times, turn, [k1, p1] 7(8:8:9) times, k1(0:1:0).

Rep the last 2 rows once more.

Bind off in rib.

Leave center 33(35:37:39) sts on a holder.

Front

Work even until front measures 2¾(3½:4¾:6¼)in/ 7(9:12:16)cm from cast-on edge, ending with a wrong side row, inc one st at center of last row.

80(86:92:98) sts.

Place anchor motif

Row 1 K23(26:29:32), work across row 1 of motif, k23(26:29:32).

Row 2 P23(26:29:32), work across row 2 of motif, p23(26:29:32).

These 2 rows set the motif position.

Working correct patt rows, cont even until front measures 6¼(7:8¼:9¾)in/16(18:21:25)cm from cast-on edge, ending with a wrong side row.

Shape armholes

Bind off 4(4:5:5) sts at beg of next 2 rows.

72(78:82:88) sts.

Next row K1, skpo, knit to last 3 sts, k2tog, k1.

Next row Purl to end.

Rep the last 2 rows 3(4:4:5) times more.

64(68:72:76) sts.

Cont in patt to end of chart.

Dec one st at center of next row, work even until front measures 9(10¼:11½:13½)in/23(26:29:34)cm from cast-on edge, ending with a wrong side row.

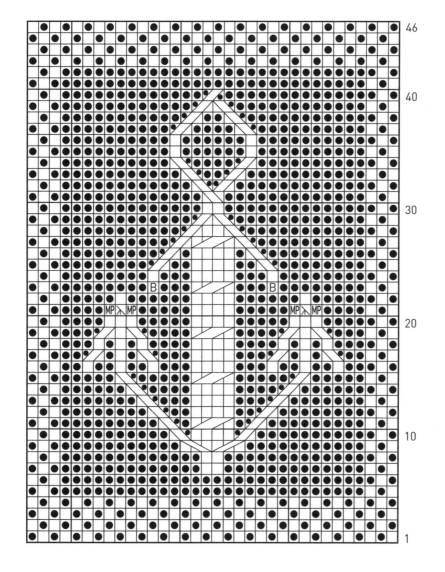

Key

☐ K on RS, P on WS

● P on RS, K on WS

◿ Sk2po

MP M1, P

B MB

◺ C2F

◺ FC

◺ BC

◺ Cr2

◿ Cr3B

◺ Cr3F

◿ C4B

Shape front neck

Row 1 K20(21:22:23), turn and work on these sts for first side on neck shaping.

Row 2 P2tog, purl to end.

Row 3 Knit to last 2 sts, k2tog.

Rep the last 2 rows once more and row 2 again. *15(16:17:18) sts.*

Work even until 5 rows less have been worked than on back to shoulder.

Shape shoulder

Rows 1 and 2 P7(8:8:9), turn, knit to end.

Buttonhole band

Row 3 [K1, p1] 7(8:8:9) times, k1(0:1:0).

Row 4 P1(0:1:0), [k1, p1] 7(8:8:9) times.

Rep the last 2 rows once more.

Buttonhole row Rib to last 5(6:7:8) sts, yo, p2tog, rib 3(4:5:6).

Work 2 rows.

Bind off in rib.

With right side facing, slip center 24(26:28:30) sts on a holder, rejoin yarn to rem sts, patt to end.

Row 2 Purl to last 2 sts, p2tog tbl.

Row 3 Skpo, knit to end.

Rep the last 2 rows once more and row 2 again. *15(16:17:18) sts.*

Work even until front measures the same as back to shoulder, ending at armhole edge.

Shape shoulder

Next row Bind off 7(8:8:9) sts, purl to end.

Work 1 row.

Bind off rem sts.

Sleeves

Using size 2 (2.75mm) needles, cast on 34(36:38:40) sts.

Next row [K1, p1] to end.

This row forms the rib.

Work 9(11:13:15) more rows.

Change to size 3 (3.25mm) needles.

Beg with a knit row, cont in St st.

Work 2 rows.

Inc row K3, m1, knit to last 3 sts, m1, k3.

Work 3 rows.

Rep the last 4 rows 10(11:14:15) times more and the inc row again. *58(62:70:74) sts.*

Cont straight until sleeve measures 6¾(8¼:9¾:11½)in/ 17(21:25:29cm from cast-on edge, ending with a wrong side row.

Shape top

Bind off 4(4:5:5) sts at beg of next 2 rows. *50(54:60:64) sts.*

Next row K1, skpo, knit to last 3 sts, k2tog, k1.

Next row Purl to end.

Rep the last 2 rows 3(3:4:4) times more. *42(46:50:54) sts.*

Bind off.

Neckband

Join right shoulder seam.

With right side facing, size 2 (2.75mm) needles, pick up and k16(16:18:18) sts down left side of front neck, k24(26:28:30) sts from front neck holder, dec one st at center, pick up and k16(16:18:18) sts up right side of front neck, k33(35:37:39) sts from back neck, then pick up and k5 sts along buttonband. *93(97:105:109) sts.*

Rib row 1 K2, [p1, k1] to last 3 sts, p1, k2.

Rib row 2 K1, [p1, k1] to end.

Buttonhole row K2, p1, s2kpo, rib to last 5 sts, p2tog, yo, p1, k2.

Rib 2 rows.

Bind off in rib.

Finishing

Sew on sleeves. Join side and sleeve seams. Sew on buttons.

lotte cardigan

Cute birds parade around this cropped, box-shaped cardigan, interspersed with traditional Scandinavian snowflake motifs. The shawl collar, hem, and cuffs are knitted in seed stitch. Knitted in *Rowan Fine Tweed*.

Sizes

To fit ages

| 6–9 | 12–18 | 24–36 | 36–48 | months |

Actual measurements

Chest

| 21½ | 23¼ | 24¾ | 26¼ | in |
| 55 | 59 | 63 | 67 | cm |

Length to shoulder

| 8¾ | 10 | 11½ | 13½ | in |
| 22 | 25 | 29 | 34 | cm |

Sleeve length

| 6¾ | 8¼ | 9¾ | 11½ | in |
| 17 | 21 | 25 | 29 | cm |

Yarns

Rowan Fine Tweed

5(5:6:6) x 1oz/98yd balls Buckden 364 (M)

One ball each Askrigg 365 (A), Skipton 379 (B), and Richmond 381 (C)

Needles

Pair each of size 2/3 (3mm) and size 3 (3.25mm) knitting needles

Circular size 2/3 (3mm) and size 3 (3.25mm) needle

Extras

4(4:5:6) buttons

Gauge

28 sts and 34 rows to 4in/10cm square over patt using size 3 (3.25mm) needles, *or size to obtain correct gauge.*

Abbreviations

See page 141.

Note

When working from Charts, right side rows are read from right to left and wrong side rows from left to right. Use the Fairisle method, strand the yarn not in use across the wrong side of work, weaving them under and over the working yarn every 3 or 4 sts.

Back and Fronts

(worked in one piece to armholes)

Using size 2/3 (3mm) circular needle and M, cast on 165(191:191:207) sts.

Seed st row (RS) K1, [p1, k1] to end.

This row forms the seed st.

Work a further 5(7:9:11) rows.

Change to size 3 (3.25mm) circular needle.

Beg with a knit row, work in St st.

Work 2 rows.

Work rows 1–8 from Chart 1.

Using M, work 2(4:6:8) rows, inc(dec:dec:inc) 1(1:1:7) st(s) evenly across last row. *166(190:190:214) sts.*

Work in patt from Chart 2.

Row 1 K1M, [work row 1 of Chart, k4M] 6(7:7:8) times, work row 1 of Chart, k1M.

Row 2 P1M, [work row 2 of Chart, p4M] 6(7:7:8) times, work row 2 of Chart, p1M.

These 2 rows set the patt.

Cont in patt to end of row 17.

Next row Using M, purl to end, inc dec st at center of row. *165(189:189:213) sts.*

Using M, work 1(3:5:7) row(s) St st.

Next row P4M, [1B, 5M] to last 5 sts, 1B, 4M.

Next row K3M, [1B, 1M, 1B, 3M] to end.

Next row P4M, [1B, 5M] to last 5 sts, 1B, 4M.

Dec row Using M, k7(5:4:7) [k2tog, k13(6:16:6)] 10(22:10: 22) times, k2tog, k6(6:3:6). *154(166:178:190) sts.*

Using M, work 1(1:5:13) row(s) St st.

Divide for back and fronts

Next row K34(36:38:40), leave these sts on a spare needle for right front, bind off 7(9:11:13) sts, knit next 71(75:79:83) sts, leave these72(76:80:84) sts on a spare needle for back, bind off 7(9:11:13) sts, knit to end.

Cont on these 34(36:38:40) sts for left front.

Next row P4M, [1B, 5M] to last 6(8:4:6) sts, 1B, 5(7:3:5)M.

Next row K4(6:2:4) M, [1B, 1M, 1B, 3M] to end.

Chart 1

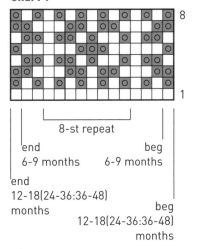

8-st repeat

end
6-9 months

beg
6-9 months

end
12-18(24-36:36-48)
months

beg
12-18(24-36:36-48)
months

Chart 3

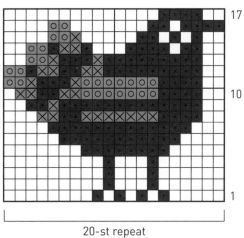

20-st repeat

Chart 2

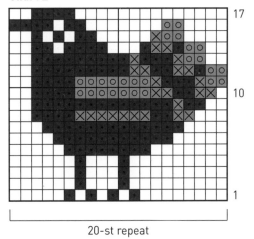

20-st repeat

Chart 4

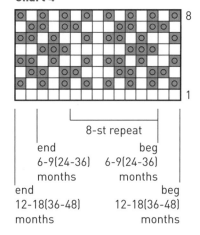

8-st repeat

end
6-9(24-36)
months

beg
6-9(24-36)
months

end
12-18(36-48)
months

beg
12-18(36-48)
months

Key

☐ Buckden (M)

■ Askrigg (A)

▣ Skipton (B)

☒ Richmond (C)

Next row P4M, [1B, 5M] to last 6(8:4:6) sts, 1B, 5(7:3:5)M.

Using M, work 1(3:5:7) row(s).

Work in patt from Chart 3.

Row 1 P7(8:9:10)M, work row 1 of Chart, p7(8:9:10)M.

Row 2 K7(8:9:10)M, work row 2 of Chart, k7(8:9:10)M.

These 2 rows set the patt.

Cont in patt to end of row 17.

Using M, work 1(3:5:7) row(s).

Next row P4M, [1B, 5M] to last 6(8:4:6) sts, 1B, 5(7:3:5)M.

Next row K4(6:2:4)M, [1B, 1M, 1B, 3M] to end.

Next row P4M, [1B, 5M] to last 6(8:4:6) sts, 1B, 5(7:3:5)M.

Cont in M only.

Shape neck

Row 1 Knit to last 3 sts, k2tog, k1.

Row 2 P1, p2tog, purl to end.

Dec one st at neck edge as set, on the next 10(11:12:13) rows. *22(23:24:25) sts.*

Work 2(3:4:5) rows.

Shape upper arm

Bind off 4 sts at beg of next and 2 foll right side rows. *10(11:12:13) sts.*

Work 1 row.

Next row Bind off 5 sts, knit to end.

Work 1 row.

Bind off rem 5(6:7:8) sts.

Back

With wrong side facing, rejoin yarn to center 72(76:80:84) sts, cast on one st. *73(77:81:85) sts.*

Next row P3(5:4:6)M, [1B, 5M] to last 4(6:5:7) sts, 1B, 3(5:4:6)M.

Next row K2(4:3:5) M, [1B, 1M, 1B, 3M] to last 5(7:6:8) sts, 1B, 1M, 1B, 2(4:3:5) M.

Next row P3(5:4:6)M, [1B, 5M] to last 4(6:5:7) sts, 1B, 3(5:4:6)M.

Using M, work 1(3:5:7) row(s).

Work in patt from Chart 3.

Next row P8(9:10:11)M, work row 1 of Chart,

p17(19:21:23)M, work row 1 of Chart, p8(9:10:11)M.

Next row K8(9:10:11)M, work row 2 of Chart, k17(19:21:23)M, work row 2 of Chart, k8(9:10:11)M.

These 2 rows set the motif.

Cont in patt to end of row 17.

Using M, work 1(3:5:7) row(s).

Next row P3(5:4:6)M, [1B, 5M] to last 4(6:5:7) sts, 1B, 3(5:4:6)M.

Next row K2(4:3:5) M, [1B, 1M, 1B, 3M] to last 5(7:6:8) sts, 1B, 1M, 1B, 2(4:3:5) M.

Next row P3(5:4:6)M, [1B, 5M] to last 4(6:5:7) sts, 1B, 3(5:4:6)M.

Cont in M only.

Work 14(16:18:20) rows.

Shape upper arms

Bind off 4 sts at beg of next 6 rows. *49(53:57:61) sts.*

Shape shoulders

Bind off 5 sts at beg of next 2 rows and and 5(6:7:8) sts at beg of foll 2 rows.

Leave rem 29(31:33:35) sts on a spare needle.

Right front

With wrong side facing, rejoin yarn to rem 34(36:38:40) sts.

Next row P5(7:3:5)M, [1B, 5M] to last 5 sts, 1B, 4M.

Next row K3M, [1B, 1M, 1B, 3M] to last 7(9:5:7) sts, 1B, 1M, 1B, 4(6:2:4)M.

Next row P5(7:3:5)M, [1B, 5M] to last 5 sts, 1B, 4M.

Using M, work 1(3:5:7) row(s).

Work in patt from Chart 3.

Row 1 P7(8:9:10)M, work row 1 of Chart, p7(8:9:10)M.

Row 2 K7(8:9:10)M, work row 2 of Chart, k7(8:9:10)M.

These 2 rows set the patt.

Cont in patt to end of row 17.

Using M, work 1(3:5:7) row(s).

Next row P5(7:3:5)M, [1B, 5M] to last 5 sts, 1B, 4M.

Next row K3M, [1B, 1M, 1B, 3M] to last 7(9:5:7) sts, 1B, 1M, 1B, 4(6:2:4)M.

Next row P5(7:3:5)M, [1B, 5M] to last 5 sts, 1B, 4M.

Cont in M only.

Shape neck

Row 1 K1, skpo, knit to end.

Row 2 Purl to last 3 sts, p2tog tbl, p1.

Dec one st at neck edge as set on the next 10(11:12:13) rows. *22(23:24:25) sts.*

Work 3(4:5:6) rows.

Shape upper arm

Bind off 4 sts at beg of next and 2 foll wrong side rows. *10 (11:12:13) sts.*

Shape shoulder

Work 1 row.

Next row Bind off 5 sts, purl to end.

Work 1 row.

Bind off rem 5(6:7:8) sts.

Sleeves

Using size 2/3 (3mm) needles and M, cast on *43(47:51:55) sts.*

Seed st row (RS) K1, [p1, k1] to end.

This row forms the seed st.

Work a further 5(7:9:11) rows

Change to size 3 (3.25mm) needles.

Beg with a knit row, work in St st.

Work 2 rows.

Work rows 1–8 from Chart 4.

Using M work 2 rows, inc one st at center of last row. *44(48:52:56) sts.*

Place motif

Row 1 K12(14:16:18)M, work across row 1 of Chart 2, k12(14:16:18)M.

Row 2 P12(14:16:18)M, work across row 2 of Chart 2, p12(14:16:18)M.

These 2 rows set the position for the Chart.

Cont in patt at the same time, inc one st at each end of the next and 3 foll 4th rows. *52(56:60:64) sts.*

Work 3 rows to complete Chart.

Cont in M only, inc one st at each end on next and every foll 10th row until there are 58(64:70:76) sts.

Work even until sleeve measures 6¾(8¼:9¾:11½)in/ 17(21:25:29)cm from cast-on edge, ending with a

wrong side row.

Mark each end of last row with a colored thread.

Work a further 4(6:6:8) rows.

Bind off.

Front band and Collar

Join shoulder seams.

Using size 2/3 (3mm) needles, right side facing and M, pick up and k46(54:66:80) sts up right front to beg of neck shaping, 22(24:26:28) sts to shoulder seam, then k2(3:4:5), [m1, k4] 6 times, k3(4:5:6) across back neck sts, pick up and k22(24:26:28) sts to beg of neck shaping, turn. *125(139:157:177) sts.*

Work on last 79(85:91:97) sts only.

Row 1 P1, [k1, p1] 28(30:32:34) times, turn.

This row sets the seed st.

Row 2 Seed st to last 22(24:26:28) sts, turn.

Next 2 rows Seed st to last 20(21:22:23) sts, turn.

Next 2 rows Seed st to last 18 sts, turn.

Next 2 rows Seed st to last 15 sts, turn.

Next 2 rows Seed st to last 12 sts, turn.

Next 2 rows Seed st to last 9 sts, turn.

Next 2 rows Seed st to last 6 sts, turn.

Next row Seed st to last 3 sts, turn, seed st to end, pick up and k46(54:66:80) sts to cast-on edge. *171(193:223:257) sts.*

Seed st 3 rows across all sts.

Buttonhole row Seed st 4(5:4:4), rib 2tog, yo, [rib 10(12:10:10) rib 2tog, yo] 3(3:4:5) times, seed st to end.

Work 3 rows across all sts.

Bind off in seed st.

Finishing

Join sleeve seams to colored threads. Sew in sleeves. Sew on buttons.

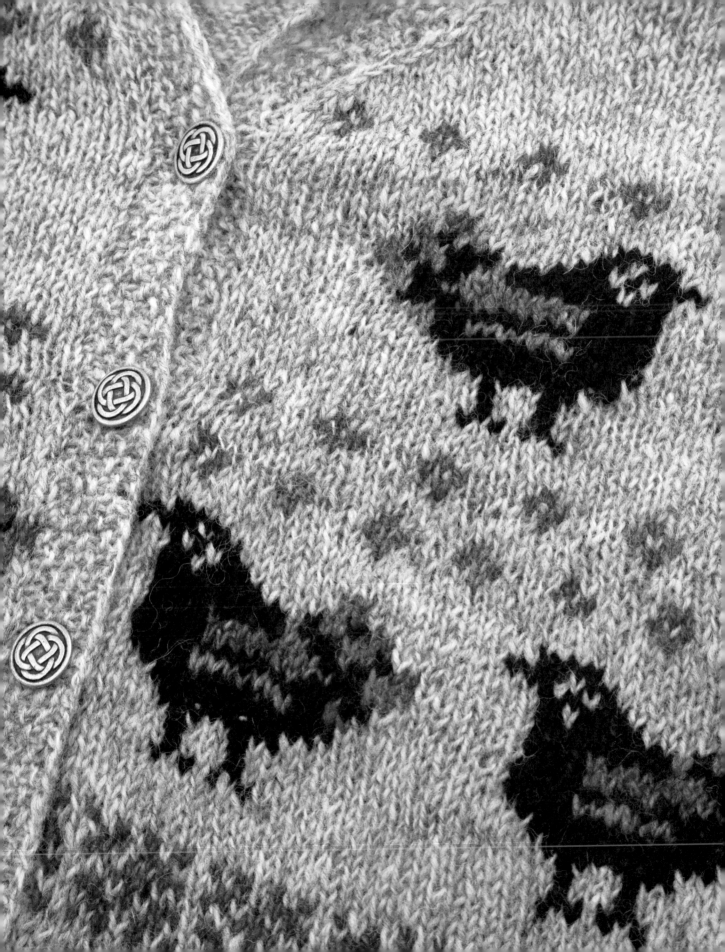

lotte scarf

The same little bird from the Lotte cardigan reappears in different colorways for this cozy but narrow scarf. Knitted in *Rowan Fine Tweed*.

Size
3in/8cm wide by 38(42:46:50)in/97(107:117:127)cm long

Yarns
Rowan Fine Tweed
3(3:4:4) x 1oz/98yd balls Nappa 380 (M)
One ball each Hubberholme 370 (A), Hawes 362 (B), and Burnsall 375

Needles
Pair of size 3 (3.25mm) knitting needles

Gauge
28 sts and 34 rows to 4in/10cm square over patt using size 3 (3.25mm) needles, *or size to obtain correct gauge.*

Abbreviations
See page 141.

Note
When working from Charts, right side rows are read from right to left and wrong side rows from left to right.

Chart 1

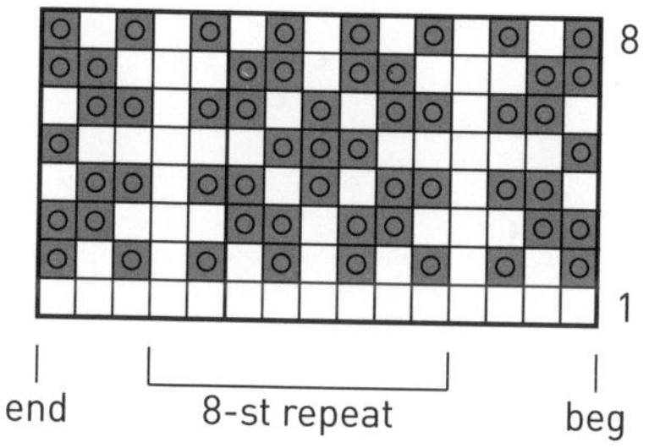

end	8-st repeat	beg

Chart 2

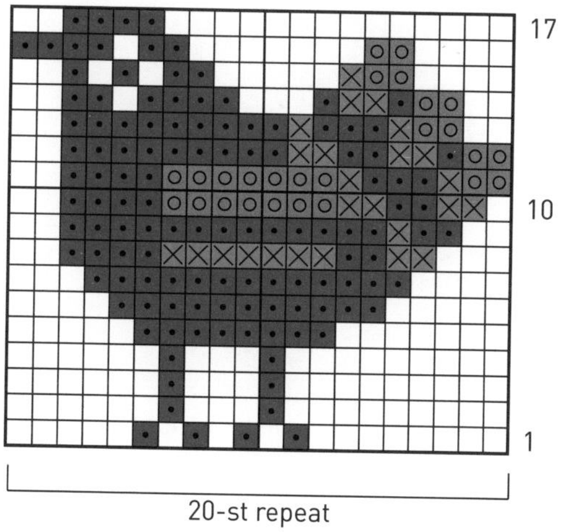

20-st repeat

Key

☐ Nappa (M)

■ Burnsall

⊙ Hubberholme (A)

⊠ Hawes (B)

To make (make 2 pieces)

Using size 3 (3.25mm) needles and M, cast on 47 sts.
Beg with a knit row, work in St st.
Work rows 1–8 from Chart 1.
Using M, work 2 rows and inc one st at center of last row. *48 sts.*
Work in patt from Chart 2.
Row 1 K2M, work row 1 of Chart, k4M, work row 1 of Chart 2, k2M.
Row 2 P2M, work row 2 of Chart, p4M, work row 2 of Chart 2, p2M.
These 2 rows set the patt.
Cont in patt to end of row 17.
Next row Using M, purl to end and dec 3 sts across row. *45 sts.*
Using M, work 1(3:5:7) row(s) St st.
Next row P4M, [1A, 5M] to last 5 sts, 1A, 4M.
Next row K3M, [1A, 1M, 1A, 3M] to end.
Next row P4M, [1A, 5M] to last 5 sts, 1A, 4M.
Cont in M only until piece measures 19(21:22¾:24¾)in/ 48(53:58:63)cm.
Leave sts on a spare needle.

Finishing

With needles pointing in the same direction and right sides together, bind off the sts of both pieces together.
Join row ends of scarf together.
With seam running down side of scarf, using size 3 (3.25mm) needles and B, working through both thicknesses, pick up and k24 sts along one short end.
Knit 2 rows.
Bind off.
Work other end to match.

sofie tunic

This very pretty tunic has a sweet heart motif on the front panel, a gently gathered skirt, and a dropped neckline. It buttons at the shoulder. Knitted in Rowan *Wool Cotton 4 Ply* yarn. It looks great with either a skirt or leggings.

Sizes

To fit ages

6–9	12–18	24–36	36–48	months

Actual measurements

Chest

21½	22¾	24¾	26	in
55	58	63	66	cm

Length to shoulder

13½	15	17	19¼	in
34	38	43	49	cm

Sleeve length

6¾	8¼	9¾	11½	in
17	21	25	29	cm

Yarn

5(5:6:6) x 1¾oz/197yd balls of Rowan *Wool Cotton 4 Ply* Violet 490

Needles

Pair each of size 2 (3mm) and size 3 (3.25mm) knitting needles
Cable needle

Extras

Stitch holders
3 buttons

Gauge

28 sts and 36 rows to 4in/10cm square over St st on size 3 (3.25mm) needles, *or size to obtain correct gauge.*

Abbreviations

K1tbl = knit through the back of the loop.

center double increase [k1tbl, k1] into next st, then insert left-hand needle point behind the vertical strand that runs downward from between the 2 sts just made and k1tbl into this strand to make the 3rd st of the group.

Cr4R = slip next st onto cable needle and hold at back of work, k3, then p1 from cable needle.

Cr4L = slip next 3 sts onto cable needle and hold at front of work, p1, then k3 from cable needle.

Cr5R = slip next 2 sts onto cable needle and hold at back of work, k3, then p2 from cable needle.

Cr5L = slip next 3 sts onto cable needle and hold at front of work, p2, then k3 from cable needle.

Dec 7 = with yarn on RS of work, slip next 4 sts, *pass the 2nd st on right-hand needle over the first (center) st, slip the center st back onto left-hand needle and pass the 2nd st on left-hand needle over it *, slip the center st back onto right-hand needle; rep from * to * twice more, knit the center st.

See also page 141.

Note

When working from Chart, right side rows are read from right to left and wrong side rows from left to right.

Back

**Using size 2 (3mm) needles, cast on 119(125:137:143) sts.

Next row K1, [p1, k1] to end.

This row forms the seed st.

Work 5 more rows.

Change to size 3 (3.25mm) needles.

Beg with a knit row, work in St st until back measures 5½(6¾:8 :10¼)in/14(17:20:26)cm from cast-on edge, ending with a knit row.

Dec row [P2tog, p1] 39(41:45:47) times, p2tog.
*79(83:91:95) sts.***

Work even until back measures 9(10¼:11¾:13¾)in/23(26:30:35)cm from cast-on edge, ending with a wrong side row.

Shape armholes

Bind off 4(4:5:5) sts at beg of next 2 rows.
71(75:81:85) sts.

Next row K1, skpo, knit to last 3 sts, k2tog, k1.

Next row Purl to end.

Rep the last 2 rows 3(3:4:4) times more.
63(67:71:75) sts.

Cont straight until back measures 13½(15:17:19¼)in/34(38:43:49)cm from cast-on edge, ending with a wrong side row.

Shape shoulders

Rows 1 and 2 Bind off 7(8:8:9) sts, knit to last 7(8:8:9) sts, turn, purl to end.

Row 3 Bind off 8(8:9:9) sts, knit to last 15(16:17:18) sts, [k1, p1] 7(8:8:9) times, k1(0:1:0).

Row 4 K1(0:1:0), [p1, k1] 7(8:8:9) times.

Row 5 [K1, p1] 7(8:8:9) times, k1(0:1:0).

Rep the last 2 rows once more.

Bind off in patt.

Leave center 33(35:37:39) sts on a holder.

Front

Work as Back from ** to **.

Work even until front measures 6¼(7½:9:11)in/16(19:23:28)cm from cast-on edge, ending with a wrong side row.

Place heart motif

Row 1 K25(27:31:33), work across row 1 of Chart, k25(27:31:33).

Row 2 P25(27:31:33), work across row 2 of Chart, p25(27:31:33).

These 2 rows set the Chart position.

Working correct patt rows, cont straight until front measures 9(10¼:11¾:13¾)in/23(26:30:35)cm from cast-on edge, ending with a wrong side row.

Shape armholes

Bind off 4(4:5:5) sts at beg of next 2 rows.

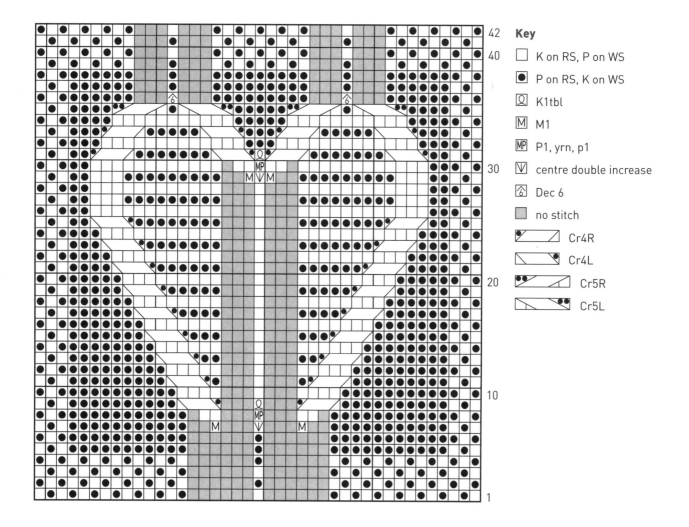

Key

☐	K on RS, P on WS
●	P on RS, K on WS
Ⓠ	K1tbl
Ⓜ	M1
ⓂⓅ	P1, yrn, p1
Ⓥ	centre double increase
⑥	Dec 6
▨	no stitch
▱	Cr4R
▱	Cr4L
▱	Cr5R
▱	Cr5L

71(75:81:85) sts.

Next row K1, skpo, patt to last 3 sts, k2tog, k1.

Next row Patt to end.

Rep the last 2 rows 3(3:4:4) times more.

63(67:71:75) sts.

Cont straight working in St st when chart is completed until front measures 11¾(13½:15:17¼)in/ 30(34:38:44)cm from cast-on edge, ending with a wrong side row.

Shape front neck

Row 1 K20(21:22:23), turn and work on these sts for first side on neck shaping.

Row 2 P2tog, purl to end.

Row 3 Knit to last 2 sts, k2tog.

Rep the last 2 rows once more and row 2 again.

15(16:17:18) sts.

Work even until 5 rows less have been worked than on back to shoulder, ending with a right side row.

Shape shoulder

Rows 1 and 2 P7(8:8:9), turn, knit to end.

Buttonhole band

Row 3 [K1, p1] 7(8:8:9) times, k1(0:1:0).

Row 4 K1(0:1:0), [p1, k1] 7(8:8:9) times.

Rep the last 2 rows once more.

Buttonhole row K1, p1, yo, k2tog, seed st 6, yo, k2tog, seed st 3(4:5:6).

Work 2 rows.

Bind off in seed st.

With right side facing, slip center 23(25:27:29) sts on a holder, rejoin yarn to rem 20(21:22:23) sts, knit to end.

Row 2 Purl to last 2 sts, p2tog tbl.

Row 3 Skpo, knit to end.

Rep the last 2 rows once more and row 2 again. *15(16:17:18) sts.*

Work even until front measures the same as back to shoulder, ending at armhole edge.

Shape shoulder

Next row Bind off 7(8:8:9) sts, purl to end.

Work 1 row.

Bind off rem sts.

Sleeves

Using size 2 (3mm) needles, cast on 31(33:37:39) sts.

Next row P1, [k1, p1] to end.

This row forms the seed st.

Work 5 more rows.

Change to size 3 (3.25mm) needles.

Beg with a knit row, cont in St st.

Work 2 rows.

Inc row K3, m1, knit to last 3 sts, m1, k3.

Work 3 rows.

Rep the last 4 rows 11(12:14:15) times more and the inc row again. *57(61:69:73) sts.*

Cont straight until sleeve measures 6¾(8¼:9¾:11½)in/ 17(21:25:29)cm from cast-on edge, ending with a wrong side row.

Shape top

Bind off 4(4:5:5) sts at beg of next 2 rows.

49(53:59:63) sts.

Next row K1, skpo, knit to last 3 sts, k2tog, k1.

Next row Purl to end.

Rep the last 2 rows 3(3:4:4) times more.

41(45:49:53) sts.

Bind off.

Neckband

Join right shoulder seam.

With right side facing, using size 2 (3mm) needles, pick up and k16(16:18:18) sts down left side of front neck, k23(25:27:29) sts from front neck holder, pick up and k16(16:18:18) sts up right side of front neck, k33(35:37:39) sts from back neck, then pick up and k5 sts along buttonband. *93(97:105:109) sts.*

Seed st row K1, [p1, k1] to end.

Rep the last row once more.

Buttonhole row K1, p1, k1, p3tog, seed st to last 5 sts, p2tog, yo, k1, p1, k1.

Seed st 2 rows.

Bind off in seed st.

Finishing

Lap buttonhole band over buttonband and baste together. Join side and sleeve seams. Sew in sleeves. Sew on buttons.

olle socks

Cozy socks in great stripes that make the most of any leftover *Felted Tweed DK* yarns, these are knitted top down on double-pointed needles.

Sizes
To fit ages

1–2	2–3	3–4	years

Yarns
1½(1¾:2)oz of leftover Rowan *Felted Tweed DK* in assorted colors

Needles
Set of 4 double-pointed needles (DPN) size 3 (3.25mm) and size 5 (3.75mm) needles
Spare needles
Stitch holder

Gauge
24 sts and 30 rows to 4in/10cm over St st using size 5 (3.75mm) needles, *or size to obtain correct gauge.*

Abbreviations
See page 141.

Note
Use the yarn for any stripe sequence you wish, we did 4 rows of each color and chose one color for the rib and heels.

Socks
Using size 3 (3.25mm) needles, cast on 40(44:48) sts. Arrange these sts on 3 needles and cont in rounds.
Rib round *K1, p1; rep from * to end.
Rib a further 5(7:9) rounds.
Change to size 5 (3.75mm) needles.
Work in stripes of 4 rows each color.
Knit 22(24:26) rounds.
Dec round K6, k2tog, knit to last 8 sts, skpo, k6.
38(42:46) sts.
Knit 7(9:11) rounds.

Dec round K5, k2tog, knit to last 7 sts, skpo, k5. *36(40:44) sts.*

Knit 7(9:11) rounds.

Dec round K4, k2tog, knit to last 6 sts, skpo, k4. *34(38:42) sts.*

Knit 7(9:11) rounds.

Dec round K3, k2tog, knit to last 5 sts, skpo, k3.

Knit 1 round. *32(36:40) sts.*

Break yarn.

Divide sts onto 3 needles as foll: slip first 9(10:11) sts onto first needle, next 7(8:9) sts onto second needle, and next 7(8:9) sts onto 3rd needle, slip last 9(10:11) sts onto other end of first needle.

Shape heel

With right side facing, join yarn to 18(20:22) sts on first needle.

Work on these 18(20:22) sts only.

Beg with a knit row, work 10 rows St st.

Next row K13(15:17), skpo, turn.

Next row Sl 1, p8(10:12), p2tog, turn.

Next row Sl 1, k8(10:12), skpo, turn.

Next row Sl 1, p8(10:12), p2tog, turn.

Rep the last 2 rows twice more. *10(12:14) sts.*

Break yarn.

Reset sts on 3 needles as foll: slip first 5(6:7) sts of heel sts onto a stitch holder, place marker here to indicate beg of round.

Rejoin yarn to rem sts, with first needle k5(6:7), then pick up and k8 sts along side of heel, with 2nd needle k14(16:18), with 3rd needle pick up and k8 sts along other side of heel, k5(6:7) from stitch holder. *40(44:48) sts.*

Cont in rounds and stripe patt.

Knit 1 round.

Dec round K11(12:13), k2tog, k14(16:18), k2tog tbl, k11(12:13). *38(42:46) sts.*

Knit 1 round.

Dec round K10(11:12), k2tog, k14(16:18), k2tog tbl, k10(11:12). *36(40:44) sts.*

Knit 1 round.

Dec round K9(10:11), k2tog, k14(16:18), k2tog tbl, k9(10:11). *34(38:42) sts.*

Knit 1 round.

Dec round K8(9:10), k2tog, k14(16:18), k2tog tbl, k8(9:10). *32(36:40) sts.*

Work 20(28:36) rounds even.

Shape toes

Dec round K5(6:7), k2tog, k2, skpo, k10(12:14), k2tog, k2, skpo, k5(6:7). *28(32:36) sts.*

Knit 1 round.

Dec round K4(5:6), k2tog, k2, skpo, k8(10:12), k2tog, k2, skpo, k4(5:6). *24(28:32) sts.*

Knit 1 round.

Dec round K3(4:5), k2tog, k2, skpo, k6(8:10), k2tog, k2, skpo, k3(4:5). *20(24:28) sts.*

Knit 1 round.

Dec round K2(3:4), k2tog, k2, skpo, k4(6:8), k2tog, k2, skpo, k2(3:4).

Knit 1 round. *16(20:24) sts.*

Slip first 4(5:6) sts onto one needle, next 8(10:12) sts onto next needle and rem 4(5:6) sts onto end of first needle.

Fold sock inside out and bind one st from each needle off together.

olle mittens

And here are the mittens to go with the socks. Fun to knit and good for using up leftover balls of yarn. Make a few pairs in case they get lost!

Sizes
To fit ages

| 1–2 | 2–3 | 3–4 | years |

Yarns
¾oz(1:1½)oz of leftover Rowan *Felted Tweed DK* in assorted colors

Needles
Pair each of size 3 (3.25mm) and size 5 (3.75mm) knitting needles

Gauge
24 sts and 30 rows to 4in/10cm over St st using size 5 (3.75mm) needles, *or size to obtain correct gauge.*

Abbreviations
See page 141.

Note
Use the yarn for any stripe sequence you wish, we did 4 rows of each color and chose one color for the rib.

Right mitt
Using size 3 (3.25mm) needles, cast on 30(34:38) sts.
Rib row [K1, p1] to end.
Rep the last row 13 times more.
Change to size 5 (3.75mm) needles.
Cont in stripes of 4 rows.
Beg with a knit row, work 4 rows in St st.
Thumb shaping
Next row K15(17:19), m1, k2, m1, k13(15:17). *32(36:40) sts.*
Work 1 row.
Next row K15(17:19), m1, k4, m1, k13(15:17). *34(38:42) sts.*
Work 1 row.

Next row K15(17:19), m1, k6, m1, k13(15:17).
36(40:44) sts.
Work 1 row.
Next row K15(17:19), m1, k8, m1, k13(15:17).
38(42:46) sts.
Work 1 row.
2nd and 3rd sizes only
Next row K(17:19), m1, k10, m1, k(15:17). *(44:48) sts.*
Work 1 row.
3rd size only
Next row K(19), m1, k12, m1, k(17).
Work 1 row.
All sizes
38(44:50) sts.
Divide for thumb
Next row K25(30:35), turn, cast on 2 sts.
Next row P11(14:17) sts, turn, cast on 2 sts.
13(16:19) sts.
St st 8(10:12) rows.
Next row K1(0:1), * skpo; rep from * to end.
Next row Purl to end.
Break yarn, thread through rem sts, draw up tightly,
and join seam.
With right side facing, pick up and k3(4:5) sts from
base of thumb, knit to end. *32(36:40) sts.***
St st 17(21:25) rows.
Shape top
Next row K2, [skpo, k9(11:13), k2tog, k2] twice.
28(32:36) sts.
Purl 1 row.
Next row K2, [skpo, k7(9:11), k2tog, k2] twice.
24(28:32) sts.
Purl 1 row.
Next row K2, [skpo, k5(7:9), k2tog, k2] twice.
20(24:28) sts.
Purl 1 row. Bind off.

Left mitt

Using size 3 (3.25mm) needles, cast on 30(34:38) sts.
Rib row [K1, p1] to end.

Rep the last row 13 times more.
Change to size 5 (3.75mm) needles.
Cont in stripes of 4 rows.
Beg with a knit row, work 4 rows in St st.
Thumb shaping
Next row K13(15:17), m1, k2, m1, k15(17:19).
32(36:40) sts.
Work 1 row.
Next row K13(15:17), m1, k4, m1, k15(17:19).
34(38:42) sts.
Work 1 row.
Next row K13(15:17), m1, k6, m1, k15(17:19).
36(40:44) sts.
Work 1 row.
Next row K13(15:17), m1, k8, m1, k15(17:19).
38(42:46) sts.
Work 1 row.
2nd and 3rd sizes only
Next row K(15:17), m1, k10, m1, k(17:19). *(44:48) sts.*
Work 1 row.
3rd size only
Next row K(17), m1, k12, m1, k(19). *50 sts.*
Work 1 row.
All sizes
38(44:50) sts.
Divide for thumb
Next row K22(26:30), turn, cast on 2 sts.
Next row P11(14:17) sts, turn, cast on 2 sts.
13(16:19) sts.
St st 8(10:12) rows.
Next row K1(0:1), * skpo; rep from * to end. *7(8:10) sts.*
Next row Purl to end.
Break yarn, thread through rem sts, draw up tightly
and join seam.
With RS facing, pick up and k3(4:5) sts from base of
thumb, knit to end. Work as given for right mitt from **
to end.

Finishing

Join seam.

alexa poncho

Great for keeping warm, a hooded poncho is really easy to wear and can be layered over other sweaters. This one, in eye-catching pink, knitted in Rowan *Wool Cotton*, is a real girly treat. It has a lovely cabled edge for a finishing detail.

Sizes

To fit ages

6–9	12–18	24–36	36–48	months

Actual measurements

Cuff to cuff

24	28	31¾	35	in
61	71	81	89	cm

Length to shoulder

11½	12½	14¼	16¼	in
29	32	36	41	cm

Yarns

7(8:9:10) x 1¾oz/123yd balls of Rowan *Wool Cotton* Flower 943

Needles

Pair each of size 3 (3.25mm) and size 6 (4mm) knitting needles
Long size 6 (4mm) circular needle
Cable needle

Gauge

22 sts and 30 rows to 4in/10cm measured over St st using size 6 (4mm) needles, *or size to obtain correct gauge.*

Abbreviations

C6B = slip next 3 sts onto cable needle and hold at back of work, k3, then k3 from cable needle.

C6F = slip next 3 sts onto cable needle and hold at front of work, k3, then k3 from cable needle.

C4R = slip next st onto cable needle and hold at back of work, k3, then p1 from cable needle.

C4L = slip next 3 sts onto cable needle and hold at front of work, p1, then k3 from cable needle.

C5R = slip next 2 sts onto cable needle and hold at back of work, k3, then p2 from cable needle.

C5L = slip next 3 sts onto cable needle and hold at front of work, p2, then k3 from cable needle.

MB = make bobble, [k1, p1, k1] all into next st, turn, p3, turn, k3, turn, p3, turn, sl 1, k2tog, psso.

C9B = slip next 4 sts onto cable needle and hold at back of work, k5, then k4 from cable needle.

See also page 141.

Note

When working from Charts, right side rows are read from right to left and wrong side rows from left to right.

Back

Using size 6 (4mm) circular needle, cast on 118(136:154:168) sts

Foundation row (WS) P33(42:51:58), k2, p3, k5, p1, k2, [p6, k4] twice, p6, k2, p1, k5, p3, k2, p33(42:51:58). Work in established patt.

Row 1 K33(42:51:58), work across row 1 of panel A, k1, panel B, k1, panel C, k33(42:51:58).

Row 2 P33(42:51:58), work across row 2 of panel C, p1, panel B, p1, panel A, p33(42:51:58).

These 2 rows set the panels and form the St st at sides. Work even until back measures 11½(12½:14¼:16¼)in/ 29(32:36:41)cm from cast-on edge, ending with a wrong side row.

Panel A

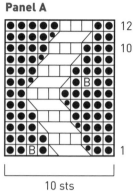

10 sts

Panel B

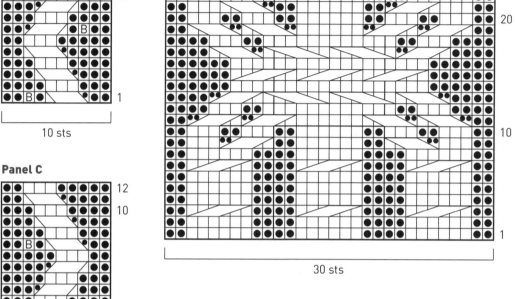

30 sts

Panel C

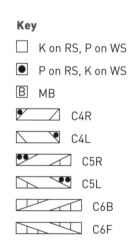

10 sts

Key

☐ K on RS, P on WS

▣ P on RS, K on WS

Ⓑ MB

C4R

C4L

C5R

C5L

C6B

C6F

Bind off 32(40:48:54) sts at beg of next 2 rows.
Bind off rem 54(56:58:60) sts, dec 6 sts over panel B.

Front

Work as given for back until front measures
8¾(9¾:11:13)in/22(25:28:33)cm from cast-on edge,
ending with a wrong side row.

Front neck shaping

Next row Patt 44(53:62:69), turn and work on these sts
for first side of neck shaping.

Next row Bind off 2 sts, patt to end.

Next row Patt to end.

Rep the last 2 rows 3(4:5:6) times more. *36(43:50:55) sts.*

Next row Work 2tog, patt to end.

Next row Patt to end.

Rep the last 2 rows 3(2:1:0) time(s) more.

32(40:48:54) sts.

Work even until front measures the same as back, ending at side edge.

Bind off.

With right side facing, rejoin yarn to rem sts, dec 6 sts evenly, bind off center 30 sts, patt to end.

Next row Patt to end.

Next row Bind off 2 sts, patt to end.

Next row Patt to end.

Rep the last 2 rows 3(4:5:6) times more.

36(43:50:55) sts.

Next row Work 2tog, patt to end.

Next row Patt to end.

Rep the last 2 rows 3(2:1:0) time(s) more.

32(40:48:54) sts.

Work even until front measures the same as back, ending at side edge.

Bind off.

Hood

Using size 6 (4mm) needles, cast on 94(102:110:118) sts.

Beg with a knit row cont in St st until work measures 8½(9:9½:10)in/22(23:24:25)cm from cast-on edge, ending with a purl row.

Shape top

Next row K47(51:55:59), turn, and work on these sts.

Next row Bind off 6 sts, purl to end.

Next row Knit to end.

Rep the last 2 rows 6 times more.

Bind off rem sts.

With right side facing, rejoin yarn to rem sts.

Next row Bind off 6 sts, knit to end.

Next row Purl to end.

Rep the last 2 rows 6 times more.

Bind off rem sts.

Cuffs

Join shoulder seams.

Place a marker 30(32:36:38) rows down from shoulder seams.

With right side facing, using size 3 (3.25mm) needles pick up and k50(54:58:62) sts between markers.

Row 1 K2, [p2, k2] to end.

Row 2 P2, [k2, p2] to end.

Rep the last 2 rows for 2¾(3¼:3½:4)in/7(8:9:10)cm ending with row 1.

Bind off in rib.

Cable trim

Using size 6 (4mm) needles, cast on 11 sts.

Row 1 (RS) P2, k9.

Row 2 P9, k2.

Row 3 and 4 As rows 1 and 2.

Row 5 P2, C9B.

Row 6 As row 2.

Rows 7–12 Rep rows 1 and 2, three times.

These 12 rows form the patt.

Cont in established patt until trim fits around entire outer edge of poncho.

Bind off.

Work a further trim to fit round edge of hood.

Finishing

Join bound-off edges of hood. Sew trim to row ends. Sew hood to neck edge. Join cuff seams. Placing cable edge at outer edge, begin and end at center back, gather edging at corners so it remains flat, slip stitch in place.

josef vest

Lots of small children like to have their arms free so this sleeveless textured short vest is just the thing to wear over a cotton shirt. Knitted in Rowan *Wool Cotton 4 Ply* with a lovely checkerboard pattern.

Sizes

To fit ages

6–9	12–18	24–36	36–48	months

Actual measurements

Chest

21½	23¼	24¾	26½	in
55	59	63	67	cm

Length to shoulder

11	12¼	13½	15	in
28	31	34	38	cm

Yarn

2(3:3:4) x 1¾oz/197yd balls of Rowan *Wool Cotton 4 Ply* Aqua 487

Needles

Pair each of size 2/3 (3mm) and size 3 (3.25mm) knitting needles
Circular size 2/3 (3mm) and size 3 (3.25mm) needles
Cable needle

Extras

4 buttons

Gauge

28 sts and 36 rows to 4in/10cm square over St st using size 3 (3.25mm) needles, *or size to obtain correct gauge.*

Abbreviations

C4F = slip next 2 sts onto cable needle and hold at front of work, k2, then k2 from cable needle.
C4R = slip next 2 sts onto cable needle and hold at back of work, k2, then p2 from cable needle.
C4L = slip next 2 sts onto cable needle and hold at front of work, p2, then k2 from cable needle.
See also page 141.

Note

When working from Chart, right side rows are read from right to left and wrong side rows from left to right.

Back and Fronts

(worked in one piece up to armholes)
Using size 2/3 (3mm) circular needle, cast on 145(157:169:181) sts.
Rib row 1 P1, [k1, p1] to end.
Rib row 2 K1, [p1, k1] to end.
Rep the last 2 rows 6(7:8:9) times more, inc one st at center of last row. *146(158:170:182) sts.*
Change to size 3 (3.25mm) circular needle.

1st and 3rd sizes only
Row 1 (RS) P1, [work 24-st patt rep] 6(-:7:-) times, p1.
Row 2 Knit to end.
These 2 rows set the patt.

2nd and 4th sizes only
Row 1 (RS) P1, [work 24-st patt rep] 6(-:7:-) times, k12, p1.
Row 2 Knit to end.
These 2 rows set the patt.

All sizes
Cont in patt until work measures 7(8:8¾:9¾)in/ 18(20:22:25)cm from cast-on edge, ending with a wrong side row.

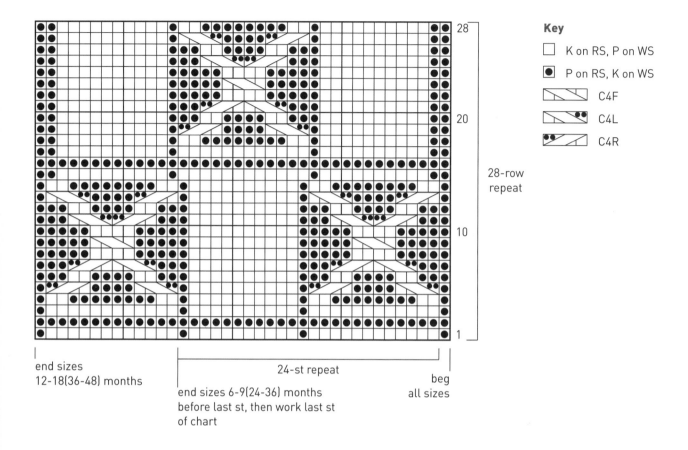

Key

- ☐   K on RS, P on WS
- ⬤   P on RS, K on WS
- ▨   C4F
- ▨   C4L
- ▨   C4R

28-row repeat

end sizes
12-18(36-48) months

24-st repeat

end sizes 6-9(24-36) months
before last st, then work last st
of chart

beg
all sizes

Divide for back and fronts

Next row Patt 31(33:35:37), leave these sts on a spare needle for right front, bind off next 10(12:14:16) sts, patt until there are 64(68:72:76) sts on the needle, turn and work on these sts for back, leave rem 41(45:49:53) sts on a spare needle for left front.

Next row Patt to end.

Next row K1, skpo, patt to last 3 sts, k2tog, k1.
Rep the last 2 rows 5 times more. *52(56:60:64) sts.*
Cont straight until work measures 11(12¼:13½:15)in/ 28(31:34:38)cm from cast-on edge, ending with a wrong side row.

Shape shoulders

Bind off 5(5:6:6) sts at beg of next 2 rows and 5(6:6:7) sts at beg of foll 2 rows.

Bind off rem 32(34:36:38) sts.

With right side facing, return to left front sts, bind off next 10(12:14:16) sts, patt to end. *31(33:35:37) sts.*

Next row Patt to end.

Next row K1, skpo, patt to last 3 sts, k2tog, k1.
Rep the last 2 rows 5 times more. *19(21:23:25) sts.*

Next row Patt to end.

Next row Patt to last 3 sts, k2tog, k1.
Rep the last 2 rows until 10(11:12:13) sts rem.
Work even until front measures the same as back to shoulder, ending at armhole edge.

Shape shoulder

Next row Bind off 5(5:6:6) sts, patt to end.
Work 1 row.
Bind off rem sts.

With wrong side facing, return to right front sts, patt to end. *31(33:35:37) sts.*

Next row K1, skpo, patt to last 3 sts, k2tog, k1.

Next row Patt to end.

Rep the last 2 rows 5 times more. *19(21:23:25) sts.*

Next row K1, skpo, patt to end.

Next row Patt to end.

Rep the last 2 rows until 10(11:12:13) sts rem.

Work even until front measures the same as back to shoulder, ending at armhole edge.

Shape shoulder

Next row Bind off 5(5:6:6) sts, patt to end.

Work 1 row.

Bind off rem sts.

Right front band and Collar

Using size 3 (3.25mm) circular needle, right side facing, pick up and k54(59:64:72) sts to beg of neck shaping, 45(48:51:57) sts to shoulder seam, then cast on 24(24:26:26) sts. *123(131:141:155) sts.*

Next 2 rows P1, [k1, p1] 12 times, turn, rib to end.

Next 2 rows Rib 29, turn, rib to end.

Next 2 rows Rib 33, turn, rib to end.

Next 2 rows Rib 37, turn, rib to end.

Next 2 rows Rib 41, turn, rib to end.

Next 2 rows Rib 45, turn, rib to end.

Cont in this way, working 4 more sts on each turning row for a further 12(14:14:16) rows.

Work 9 rows across all sts.

Bind off in rib.

Left front band and Collar

Using size 3 (3.25mm) circular needle, cast on 24(24:26:26) sts, then with right side facing, pick up and k45(48:51:57) sts to beg of neck shaping, 54(59:64:72) sts to cast-on edge. *123(131:141:155) sts.*

1st row P1, [k1, p1] to end.

This row sets the rib.

Next 2 rows Rib 25, turn, rib to end.

Next 2 rows Rib 29, turn, rib to end.

Next 2 rows Rib 33, turn, rib to end.

Next 2 rows Rib 37, turn, rib to end.

Next 2 rows Rib 41, turn, rib to end.

Next 2 rows Rib 45, turn, rib to end.

Cont in this way working 4 more sts on each turning row for a further 12(14:14:16) rows.

Work 3 rows across all sts.

Buttonhole row Rib 4, rib 2tog, y2o, rib 2tog, [rib 8(8:10:12) rib 2tog, y2o, rib 2tog] 3 times, rib to end.

Work 4 rows across all sts.

Bind off in rib.

Armbands

Join shoulder seams.

With right side facing, using size 2/3 (3mm) needles, pick up and k74(80:86:98) sts evenly round armhole edge.

Rib row [K1, p1] to end.

Rep the last row 4 times more.

Bind off in rib.

Finishing

Sew row ends of back collar, sew cast-on edge to bound-off edge at back neck. Join side seams. Sew on buttons.

alphabet throw

Instant nostalgia comes with this lovely alphabet throw with traditional letters interspersed with reindeer and heart motifs. Knitted in Rowan *Felted Tweed DK* for a soft, cozy feel.

Size

23¾in/60cm x 41½in/105cm

Yarns

One 1¾oz/191yd ball each of Rowan *Felted Tweed DK* Treacle 145, Rage 150, Bilberry 151, Watery 152, Phantom 153, Ginger 154, Pine 158, Gilt 160, Avocado 161, Seafarer 170, Clay 177, Horizon 179, Mineral 181, Peony 183

Needles

Pair of size 5 (3.75mm) knitting needles

Gauge

23 sts and 32 rows to 4in/10cm square over St st using size 5 (3.75mm) needles, *or size to obtain correct gauge.*

Abbreviations

See page 141.

Note

When working from Stag Chart, use the intarsia method. Use a small separate ball of yarn for each area of color, twisting the yarns on wrong side when changing color to avoid a hole.

When working from Heart and letter Charts, use the Fairisle method, strand the yarn not in use across the wrong side of work weaving them under and over the working yarn every 3 or 4 sts.

When working from Charts, right side rows are read from right to left and wrong side rows from left to right.

Motifs

Motif A (use 160 for letter)
Using size 5 (3.75mm) needles and 150, cast on 35 sts.
Row 1 K1, [p1, k1] to end.
Row 2 K1, [p1, k1] to end.
Row 3 K1, p1, k31, p1, k1.
Row 4 K1, purl to last st, k1.
These 2 rows form the St st with seed st borders.
Rows 5–15 Work as set.
Row 16 K1, p8, work across row 1 of motif, p8, k1.
Row 17 K1, p1, k7, work across row 2 of motif, k7, p1, k1.
Rows 18–32 Work from chart as set.
Row 33 K1, p1, k31, p1, k1.
Row 34 K1, purl to last st, k1.
Rows 35–45 Work as set.
Row 46 K1, [p1, k1] to end.
Row 47 K1, [p1, k1] to end.
Bind off in seed st.

Motif B (use 152 for letter)
Using size 5 (3.75mm) needles and 153, cast on 35 sts.
Row 1 K1, [p1, k1] to end.
Row 2 K1, [p1, k1] to end.
Row 3 K1, p1, k31, p1, k1.
Row 4 K1, purl to last st, k1.
These 2 rows form the St st with seed st borders.
Rows 5–15 Work as set.
Row 16 K1, p10, work across row 1 of motif, p10, k1.
Row 17 K1, p1, k9, work across row 2 of motif, k9, p1, k1.
Rows 18–32 Work from chart as set.
Row 33 K1, p1, k31, p1, k1.
Row 34 K1, purl to last st, k1.
Rows 35–45 Work as set.
Row 46 K1, [p1, k1] to end.
Row 47 K1, [p1, k1] to end.
Bind off in seed st.

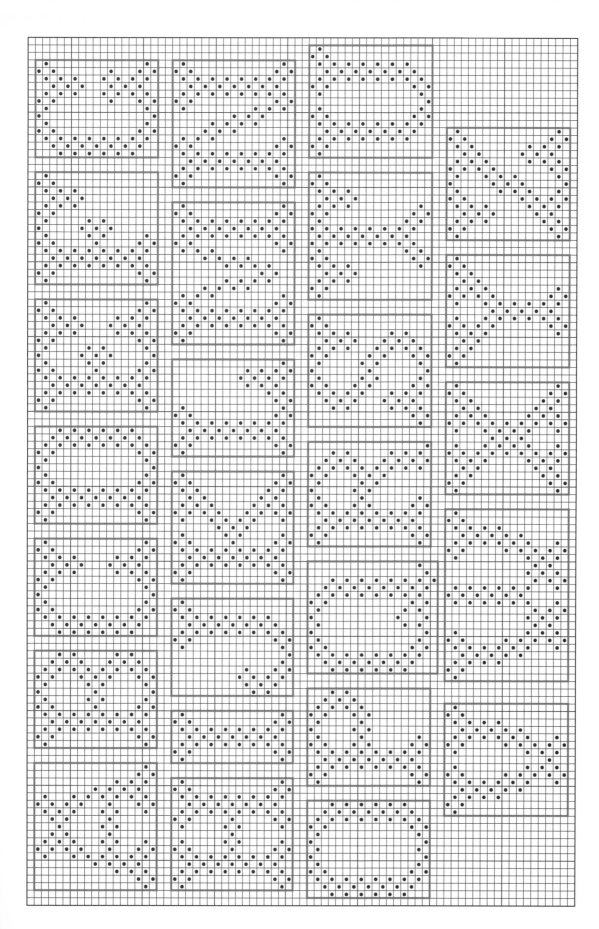

Key

☐ background colour

⦿ pattern colour

Motif C (use 170 for letter)
Using size 5 (3.75mm) needles and 177, cast on 35 sts.
Work as given for motif B.

Motif D (use 177 for letter)
Using size 5 (3.75mm) needles and 152, cast on 35 sts.
Work as given for motif B.

Motif E (use 181 for letter)
Using size 5 (3.75mm) needles and 170, cast on 35 sts.
Row 1 K1, [p1, k1] to end.
Row 2 K1, [p1, k1] to end.
Row 3 K1, p1, k31, p1, k1.
Row 4 K1, purl to last st, k1.
These 2 rows form the St st with seed st borders.
Rows 5–15 Work as set.
Row 16 K1, p9, work across row 1 of motif, p9, k1.
Row 17 K1, p1, k8, work across row 2 of motif, k8, p1, k1.
Rows 18–32 Work from chart as set.
Row 33 K1, p1, k31, p1, k1.
Row 34 K1, purl to last st, k1.
Rows 35–45 Work as set.
Row 46 K1, [p1, k1] to end.
Row 47 K1, [p1, k1] to end.
Bind off in seed st.

Motif F (use 145 for letter)
Using size 5 (3.75mm) needles and 183, cast on 35 sts.
Work as given for motif E.

Motif G (use 158 for letter)
Using size 5 (3.75mm) needles and 160, cast on 35 sts.
Work as given for motif B.

Motif H (use 145 for letter)
Using size 5 (3.75mm) needles and 161, cast on 35 sts.
Work as given for motif E.

Motif I (use 177 for letter)
Using size 5 (3.75mm) needles and 154, cast on 35 sts.

Row 1 K1, [p1, k1] to end.
Row 2 K1, [p1, k1] to end.
Row 3 K1, p1, k31, p1, k1.
Row 4 K1, purl to last st, k1.
These 2 rows form the St st with seed st borders.
Rows 5–15 Work as set.
Row 16 K1, p13, work across row 1 of motif, p13, k1.
Row 17 K1, p1, k12, work across row 2 of motif, k12, p1, k1.
Rows 18–32 Work from chart as set.
Row 33 K1, p1, k31, p1, k1.
Row 34 K1, purl to last st, k1.
Rows 35–45 Work as set.
Row 46 K1, [p1, k1] to end.
Row 47 K1, [p1, k1] to end.
Bind off in seed st.

Motif J (use 150 for letter)
Using size 5 (3.75mm) needles and 177, cast on 35 sts.
Work as given for motif B.

Motif K (use 183 for letter)
Using size 5 (3.75mm) needles and 151, cast on 35 sts.
Work as given for motif E.

Motif L (use 181 for letter)
Using size 5 (3.75mm) needles and 158, cast on 35 sts.
Work as given for motif B.

Motif M (use 170 for letter)
Using size 5 (3.75mm) needles and 179, cast on 35 sts.
Row 1 K1, [p1, k1] to end.
Row 2 K1, [p1, k1] to end.
Row 3 K1, p1, k31, p1, k1.
Row 4 K1, purl to last st, k1.
These 2 rows form the St st with seed st borders.
Rows 5–15 Work as set.
Row 16 K1, p7, work across row 1 of motif, p7, k1.
Row 17 K1, p1, k6, work across row 2 of motif, k6, p1, k1.
Rows 18–32 Work from chart as set.

Row 33 K1, p1, k31, p1, k1.
Row 34 K1, purl to last st, k1.
Rows 35–45 Work as set.
Row 46 K1, [p1, k1] to end.
Row 47 K1, [p1, k1] to end.
Bind off in seed st.

Motif N (use 160 for letter)
Using size 5 (3.75mm) needles and 150, cast on 35 sts.
Work as given for motif A.

Motif O (use 152 for letter)
Using size 5 (3.75mm) needles and 153, cast on 35 sts.
Work as given for motif B.

Motif P (use 170 for letter)
Using size 5 (3.75mm) needles and 177, cast on 35 sts.
Work as given for motif B.

Motif Q (use 177 for letter)
Using size 5 (3.75mm) needles and 152, cast on 35 sts.
Works rows 1–4 as motif E.
Row 15 K1, p1, k8, work across row 1 of motif, k8, p1, k1.
Row 16 K1, p9, work across row 2 of motif, p9, k1.
Row 17 K1, p1 k8, work across row 3 of motif, k8, p1, k1.
Rows 18–32 Work from Chart as set.
Complete as given for motif E.

Motif R (use 181 for letter)
Using size 5 (3.75mm) needles and 170, cast on 35 sts.
Works rows 1–15 as motif E.
Row 16 K1, p10, work across row 1 of motif, p9, k1.
Row 17 K1, p1 k8, work across row 2 of motif, k9, p1, k1.
Complete as given for motif E.

Motif S (use 145 for letter)
Using size 5 (3.75mm) needles and 183, cast on 35 sts.
Work as given for motif E.

Motif T (use 158 for letter)
Using size 5 (3.75mm) needles and 160, cast on 35 sts.
Work as given for motif A.

Motif U (use 145 for letter)
Using size 5 (3.75mm) needles and 161, cast on 35 sts.
Work as given for motif E.

Motif V (use 177 for letter)
Using size 5 (3.75mm) needles and 154, cast on 35 sts.
Work as given for motif E.

Motif W (use 150 for letter)
Using size 5 (3.75mm) needles and 177, cast on 35 sts.
Row 1 K1, [p1, k1] to end.
Row 2 K1, [p1, k1] to end.
Row 3 K1, p1, k31, p1, k1.
Row 4 K1, purl to last st, k1.
These 2 rows form the St st with seed st borders.
Rows 5–15 Work as set.
Row 16 K1, p5, work across row 1 of motif, p5, k1.
Row 17 K1, p1, k4, work across row 2 of motif, k4, p1, k1.
Rows 18–32 Work from chart as set.
Row 33 K1, p1, k31, p1, k1.
Row 34 K1, purl to last st, k1.
Rows 35–45 Work as set.
Row 46 K1, [p1, k1] to end.
Row 47 K1, [p1, k1] to end.
Bind off in seed st.

Motif X (use 183 for letter)
Using size 5 (3.75mm) needles and 151, cast on 35 sts.
Work as given for motif E.

Motif Y (use 181 for letter)
Using size 5 (3.75mm) needles and 158, cast on 35 sts.
Work as given for motif E.

Reindeer Motif

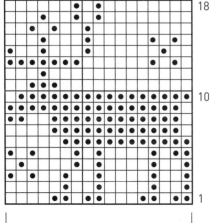

17 sts

Heart Motif

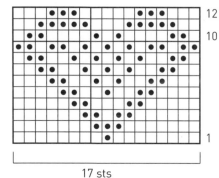

17 sts

Key

☐ background colour

⊡ pattern colour

Motif Z (use 170 for letter)
Using size 5 (3.75mm) needles and 179, cast on 35 sts.
Work as given for motif E.

Reindeer Motif (use 170 for motif)
Using size 5 (3.75mm) needles and 161, cast on 35 sts.
Row 1 K1, [p1, k1] to end.
Row 2 K1, [p1, k1] to end.
Row 3 K1, p1, k31, p1, k1.
Row 4 K1, purl to last st, k1.
These 2 rows form the St st with seed st borders.
Rows 5–13 Work as set.
Row 14 K1, p8, work across row 1 of motif, p8, k1.
Row 15 K1, p1, k7, work across row 2 of motif, k7, p1, k1.
Rows 16–31 Work from chart as set.
Row 32 K1, purl to last st, k1.
Row 33 K1, p1, k31, p1, k1.
Rows 34– 45 Work as set.
Row 46 K1, [p1, k1] to end.
Row 47 K1, [p1, k1] to end.
Bind off in seed st.

Heart Motif (use 150 for motif)
Using size 5 (3.75mm) needles and 181, cast on 35 sts.
Row 1 K1, [p1, k1] to end.
Row 2 K1, [p1, k1] to end.
Row 3 K1, p1, k31, p1, k1.
Row 4 K1, purl to last st, k1.
These 2 rows form the St st with seed st borders.
Rows 5–17 Work as set.
Row 18 K1, p8, work across row 1 of motif, p8, k1.
Row 19 K1, p1, k7, work across row 2 of motif, k7, p1, k1.
Rows 20–29 Work from chart as set.
Row 30 K1, purl to last st, k1.
Row 31 K1, p1, k31, p1, k1.
Rows 32–45 Work as set.
Row 46 K1, [p1, k1] to end.
Row 47 K1, [p1, k1] to end.
Bind off in seed st.

Finishing

Join motifs together to form a rectangle 4 squares wide by 7 squares long. Position motifs in alphabetical order with Reindeer motif between I and J and Heart motif between U and V.

alphabet blocks

The same alphabet letters, knitted in larger squares, are ideal for making a set of soft building blocks. You could make the child's name in letter blocks. Also knitted in Rowan *Felted Tweed DK*.

Size
6 x 6 x 6in/15 x 15 x 15cm

Yarns
One 1¾oz/191yd ball each of Rowan *Felted Tweed DK* Rage 150, Phantom 153, Clay 177, Gilt 160, Watery 152, Seafarer 170

Needles
Pair of size 5 (3.75mm) knitting needles

Extras
Foam blocks each 6 x 6 x 6in/15 x 15 x 15cm

Gauge
23 sts and 32 rows to 4in/10cm square over St st using size 5 (3.75mm) needles *or size to obtain correct gauge*.

Abbreviations
See page 141.

Note
When working from Charts, right side rows are read from right to left and wrong side rows from left to right.

To make
Each block is made by working six sides. We used the letters from the Alphabet Throw.

Finishing
Leaving 3 sides open, make side into a cube. Insert foam block, join remaining seams.

morten jacket

This delightful Aran-inspired, heavily cabled jacket has a warm shawl collar. The cables run up the sleeves as well as on the fronts and back. It is knitted in *Rowan Fine Tweed*.

Sizes

To fit ages

6–9	12–18	24–36	36–48	months

Actual measurements

Chest

23¼	24¾	26¾	28½	in
59	63	68	72	cm

Length to shoulder

11½	12½	14¼	16¼	in
29	32	36	41	cm

Sleeve length

6¾	8¼	9¾	11½	in
17	21	25	29	cm

Yarn

9(10:11:12) x 1oz/98yd balls of *Rowan Fine Tweed* Richmond 381

Needles

Pair of size 3 (3.25mm) knitting needles
Cable needle

Extras

4(4:5:5) buttons

Gauge

28 sts and 36 rows to 4in/10cm square over St st using size 3 (3.25mm) needles.
36 sts and 38 rows to 4in/10cm square over cable patt using size 3 (3.25mm) needles.
Or size to obtain correct gauge.

Abbreviations

Cr12fb = slip next 8 sts onto cable needle and leave at front of work, k4, then slip the last 4 sts to the left of cable needle back onto left-hand needle, take the cable needle to the back of work, k4 from left-hand needle, then k4 from cable needle.

Cr12bf = slip next 8 sts onto cable needle and leave at back of work, k4, then slip the last 4 sts to the left of cable needle, back onto left-hand needle, bring the cable needle to the front of work, k4 from left-hand needle, then k4 from cable needle.

See also page 141.

Note

When working from Chart, right side rows are read from right to left and wrong side rows from left to right.

Back

Using size 3 (3.25mm) needles, cast on 88(94:100:106) sts.

Row 1 (RS) P2(5:8:11), k4, [p2, k8, p2, k4] to last 2(5:8:11) sts, p2(5:8:11).

Row 2 K2(5:8:11), p4, [k2, p8, k2, p4], to last 2(5:2:5) sts, k2(5:8:11).

Row 3 (inc row) P2(5:8:11), k4, * p2, k1, m1, [k2, m1] 3 times, k1, p2, k4; rep from * to last 2(5:8:11) sts, p2(5:8:11). *47(50:53:56) sts.*

Row 4 K2(5:8:11), p4, [k2, p12, k2, p4] to last 2(5:8:11) sts, k2(5:8:11).

Cont in patt from chart.

Row 1 (RS) P2(5:8:11), k4, [work across row 1 of 20-st patt rep] 5 times, p2(5:8:11).

Row 2 K2(5:8:11), [work across row 2 of 20-st patt rep] 5 times, p4, k2(5:8:11).

These 2 rows **set** the cable panels.

Work even until back measures 6¼(7:8¼:9¾)in/ 16(18:21:25)cm from cast-on edge, ending with a wrong side row.

Shape armholes

Bind off 1(2:3:4) st(s) at beg of next 2 rows.

106(110:114:118) sts.

Work even until back measures 11½(12½:14¼:16¼)in/ 29(32:36:41)cm from cast-on edge, ending with a wrong side row.

Shape shoulders

Bind off 10 sts at beg of next 4 rows and 10(11:12:13) sts at beg of foll 2 rows.

Bind off rem 46(48:50:52) sts.

Left front

Using size 3 (3.25mm) needles, cast on 39(42:45:48) sts.

Row 1 (RS) P2(5:8:11), k4, [p2, k8, p2, k4] to last st, p1.

Row 2 K1, p4, [k2, p8, k2, p4], to last 2(5:8:11) sts, k2(5:8:11).

Row 3 (inc row) P2(5:8:11), k4, * p2, k1, m1, [k2, m1] 3 times, k1, p2, k4; rep from * to last st, p1. *47(50:53:56) sts.*

Row 4 K1, p4, [k2, p12, k2, p4] to last 2(5:8:11) sts, k2(5:8:11).

Cont in patt from chart.

Row 1 (RS) P2(5:8:11), k4, [work across row 1 of 20-st patt rep] twice, p1.

Row 2 K1, [work across row 2 of 20-st patt rep] twice, p4, k2(5:8:11).

These 2 rows **set** the cable panels.

Work even until front measures 6¼(7:8¼:9¾)in/ 16(18:21:25)cm from cast-on edge, ending with a wrong side row.

Shape armhole and front neck

Next row Bind off 1(2:3:4) st(s), patt to last 3 sts, work 2tog, k1. *45(47:49:51) sts.*

Work 2 rows.

Next row K1, work 2tog, patt to end.

Work 2 rows.

Next row Patt to last 3 sts, work 2tog, k1.

Cont to dec in this way on every 3rd row until 30(31:32:33) sts rem.

Work even until front measures same as back to shoulder, ending at armhole edge.

Shape shoulder

Bind off 10 sts at beg of next and foll right side row.

Work 1 row.

Bind off rem sts.

Right front

Using size 3 (3.25mm) needles, cast on 39(42:45:48) sts.

Row 1 (RS) P1, k4, [p2, k8, p2, k4] to last 2(5:8:11) sts, p2(5:8:11).

Row 2 K2(5:8:11), p4, [k2, p8, k2, p4], to last st, k1.

Row 3 (inc row) P1, k4, * p2, k1, m1, [k2, m1] 3 times, k1, p2, k4; rep from * to last 2(5:8:11) sts, p2(5:8:11). *47(50:53:56) sts.*

Row 4 K2(5:8:11), p4, [k2, p12, k2, p4] to last st, k1.

Cont in patt from chart.

Row 1 (RS) P1, [work across row 1 of 20-st patt rep] twice, k4, p2(5:8:11).

Row 2 K2(5:8:11), p4, [work across row 2 of 20-st patt rep] twice, k1.

These 2 rows **set** the cable panels.

Work even until front measures 6¼(7:8¼:9¾)in/ 16(18:21:25)cm from cast-on edge, ending with a wrong side row.

Shape armhole and front neck

Next row K1, work 2tog, patt to end.

Next row Bind off 1(2:3:4) st(s) patt to end. *45(47:49:51) sts.*

Work 1 row.

Next row Patt to last 3 sts, work 2tog, k1.

Work 2 rows.

Next row K1, work 2tog, patt to end.

Work 2 rows.

Cont to dec in this way on every 3rd row until 30(31:32:33) sts rem.

Work even until front measures same as back to shoulder, ending at armhole edge.

Shape shoulder

Bind off 10 sts at beg of next and foll wrong side row.

Work 1 row.

Bind off rem 10(11:12:13) sts.

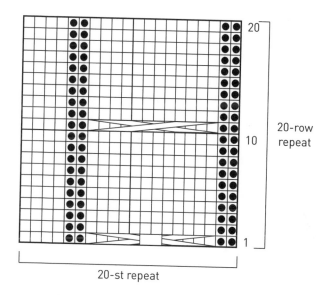

20-row repeat

20-st repeat

Key

☐ K on RS, P on WS

⬤ P on RS, K on WS

Cr12bf

Cr12fb

Sleeves

Using size 3 (3.25mm) needles, cast on 56(60:64:68) sts.

Row 1 (RS) P2(4:6:8), k4, [p2, k8, p2, k4] to last 2(4:6:8) sts, p2(4:6:8).

Row 2 K2(4:6:8), p4, [k2, p8, k2, p4], to last 2(4:6:8) sts, k2(4:6:8).

Row 3 (inc row) P2(4:6:8), k4, * p2, k1, m1, [k2, m1] 3 times, k1, p2, k4; rep from * to last 2(4:6:8) sts, p2(4:6:8). *68(72:76:80) sts.*

Row 4 K2(4:6:8), p4, [k2, p12, k2, p4] to last 2(4:6:8) sts, k2(4:6:8).

Cont in patt from chart.

Row 1 (RS) P2(4:6:8), k4, [work across row 1 of 20-st patt rep] 3 times, p2(4:6:8).

Row 2 K2(4:6:8), [work across row 2 of 20-st patt rep] 3 times, p4, k2(4:6:8).

These 2 rows **set** the cable panels.

Work a further 2(6:10:14) rows.

Inc row P2(4:6:8), m1, patt to last 2(4:6:8) sts, m1, p2(4:6:8).

Work 9 rows.

Rep the last 10 rows 3(4:4:5) times more and the inc row again, working all inc sts into rev St st. *78(84:88:94) sts.*

Work even until sleeve measures 6¾(8¼:9¾:11½)in/ 17(21:25:29)cm from cast-on edge, ending with a wrong side row.

Mark each end of last row with a colored thread.

Work a further 2(2:4:4) rows.

Bind off.

Right front band and Collar

Using size 3 (3.25mm) needles, right side facing, pick up and k45(51:57:67) sts to beg of neck shaping, 37(40:43:46) sts to shoulder seam, then cast on 16(19:22:25) sts. *98(110:122:138) sts.*

1st row P2, [k2, p2] 4(5:5:6) times, turn, rib to end.

Next 2 rows Rib 22(26:26:30), turn, rib to end.

Next 2 rows Rib 26(30:30:34), turn, rib to end.

Next 2 rows Rib 30(34:34:38), turn, rib to end.

Next 2 rows Rib 34(38:38:42), turn, rib to end.

Next 2 rows Rib 38(42:42:46), turn, rib to end.

Cont in this way working 4 more sts on each turning row for a further 6(8:10:12) rows.

Work 13 rows across all sts.

Bind off in rib.

Left front band and Collar

With size 3 (3.25mm) needles, cast on 16(19:22:25) sts, then with right side facing, pick up and k37(40:43:46) sts to beg of neck shaping, 45(51:57:67) sts to cast-on edge. *98(110:122:138) sts.*

1st row P2, [k2, p2] to end.

This row sets the rib.

Next 2 rows Rib 18(22:22:26), turn, rib to end.

Next 2 rows Rib 22(26:26:30), turn, rib to end.

Next 2 rows Rib 26(30:30:34), turn, rib to end.

Next 2 rows Rib 30(34:34:38), turn, rib to end.

Next 2 rows Rib 34(38:38:42), turn, rib to end.

Next 2 rows Rib 38(42:42:46), turn, rib to end.

Cont in this way working 4 more sts on each turning row for a further 6(8:10:12) rows.

Work 5 rows across all sts.

Buttonhole row Rib 4, rib 2tog, y2o, rib 2tog, [rib 8(10:8:10) rib 2tog, y2o, rib 2tog] 3(3:4:4) times, rib to end.

Work 6 rows across all sts.

Bind off in rib.

Finishing

Join row ends of collar. Sew collar to back neck. Sew in sleeves with last 2(2:4:4) rows to sts bound off at underarm. Join side and sleeve seams. Sew on buttons.

mikal slipover

Another great textured design, this time with a split neck, which lends itself to layering. It is knitted in Rowan *Wool Cotton*.

Sizes

To fit ages

6–9	12–18	24–36	36–48	months

Actual measurements

Chest

21¼	22¾	25	26¾	in
55	58	64	68	cm

Length to shoulder

11	12¼	13½	15	in
28	31	34	38	cm

Yarn

2(3:3:4) x 1¾oz/123yd balls of Rowan *Wool Cotton* Cypress 968

Needles

Pair each of size 3 (3.25mm) and size 6 (4mm) knitting needles

Extras

Stitch holders

2 buttons

Gauge

25 sts and 30 rows to 4in/10cm square over St st using size 6 (4mm) needles, *or size to obtain correct gauge.*

Abbreviations

K1tbl = knit through the back of the loop.

P1tbl = purl through the back of the loop.

See also page 141.

Note

When working from Chart, right side rows are read from right to left and wrong side rows from left to right.

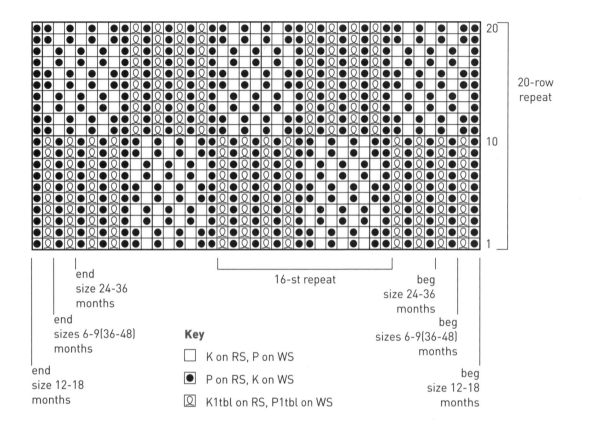

20-row repeat

10

1

end
size 24-36
months

end
sizes 6-9(36-48)
months

end
size 12-18
months

16-st repeat

beg
size 24-36
months

beg
sizes 6-9(36-48)
months

beg
size 12-18
months

Key

☐   K on RS, P on WS

●   P on RS, K on WS

Ⓠ   K1tbl on RS, P1tbl on WS

Back

Using size 3 (3.25mm) needles, cast on 69(73:81:85) sts.

Rib row 1 P1, [k1tbl, p1] to end.

Rib row 2 K1, [p1tbl, k1] to end.

Rep the last 2 rows 6(7:8:9) times more.

Change to size 6 (4mm) needles.

Work in patt from chart until back measures
7(8:8¾:9¾)in/18(20:22:25)cm from cast-on edge,
ending with a wrong side row.

Shape armholes

Bind off 5(6:7:8) sts at beg of next 2 rows.

59(61:67:69) sts **.

Next row Skpo, patt to last 2 sts, k2tog.

Next row Patt to end.

Rep the last 2 rows 5(5:6:6) times more.

47(49:53:55) sts.

Cont even until work measures 11(12¼:13½:15)in/
28(31:34:38)cm from cast-on edge, ending with a
wrong side row.

Shape shoulders

Bind off 5(5:6:6) sts at beg of next 2 rows and 5(6:6:7)
sts at beg of foll 2 rows.

Leave rem 27(27:29:29) sts on a holder.

Front

Work as given for Back to **.

Next row Skpo, patt to last 2 sts, k2tog.

57(59:65:67) sts.

Divide for front opening

Next row Patt 25(26:29:30), turn, cast on 7 sts.

32(33:36:37) sts.

Next row P1, [k1tbl, p1] 3 times, patt to last 2 sts, k2tog.

Next row Patt to last 7 sts, [k1, p1tbl] 3 times, p1.

Rep the last 2 rows 4(4:5:5) times. *27(28:30:31) sts.*

Work even until front measures 9(9¾:11:12¼)in/ 23(25:28:31)cm from cast-on edge, ending with a wrong side row.

Shape front neck

Next row Patt 12(12:13:13), leave these sts on a holder, patt to end.

Dec one st at neck edge on every row until 10(11:12:13) sts rem.

Work even until front measures the same as back to shoulder, ending at armhole edge.

Shape shoulder

Next row Bind off 5(5:6:6) sts, patt to end.

Work 1 row.

Bind off rem 5(6:6:7) sts.

Mark position for button halfway along front band.

Work buttonhole to match marker at same time as working left front as foll:

Buttonhole row (RS) Work to last 7 sts, p1, k1tbl, p1, k2tog, yo, k1tbl, p1.

With wrong side facing, rejoin yarn to rem sts, p1, [p1tbl, k1] 3 times, patt to end. *32(33:36:37) sts.*

Next row Skpo, patt to last 7 sts, [p1, k1tbl] 3 times, p1.

Next row P1, [p1tbl, k1] 3 times, patt to end.

Rep the last 2 rows 4(4:5:5) times. *27(28:30:31) sts.*

Work even until front measures 9(9¾:11:12¼)in/ 23(25:28:31)cm from cast-on edge, ending with a wrong side row.

Shape front neck

Next row Patt to last 12(12:13:13) sts, leave these sts on a holder, turn.

Dec one st at neck edge on every row until 10(11:12:13) sts rem.

Work even until front measures the same as back to shoulder, ending at armhole edge.

Shape shoulder

Next row Bind off 5(5:6:6) sts, patt to end.

Work 1 row.

Bind off rem 5(6:6:7) sts.

Neckband

Join shoulder seams.

With right side facing, using size 3 (3.25mm) needles, place 12(12:13:13) sts from holder onto needle, pick up and k12(12:14:14) sts up right side of front neck, k27(27:29:29) sts from back neck holder, pick up and k12(12:14:14) sts down left side of front neck, patt 8(8:9:9), k2tog, yo, k1tbl, p1 from left front holder. *75(75:83:83) sts.*

Row 1 P1, [p1tbl, k1] to last 2 sts, p1tbl, p1.

Row 2 P1, [k1tbl, p1] to end.

Row 3 As row 1.

Bind off in rib.

Armbands

With right side facing, size 3 (3.25mm) needles, pick up and k60(66:72:78) sts evenly around armhole edge.

Rib row 1 [P1tbl, k1] to end.

Rib row 2 [P1, k1tbl] to end.

Work 1 more row.

Bind off in rib.

Finishing

Join side seams. Sew buttonband to back of buttonhole band. Sew on buttons.

aneka cardigan

A lovely traditional Aran cardigan for girls, this one is knitted in Rowan *Siena 4 Ply*, a cotton yarn that shows the cables and textures really beautifully as well as being easy to wear. Pretty heart buttons make a nice finishing touch.

Sizes

To fit ages

6–9	12–18	24–36	36–48	months

Actual measurements

Chest

21½	23¼	24¾	26½	in
55	59	63	67	cm

Length to shoulder

11½	12½	14¼	16¼	in
29	32	36	41	cm

Sleeve length

6¾	8¼	9¾	11½	in
17	21	25	29	cm

Yarn

4(5:5:6) x 1¾oz/153yd balls of Rowan *Siena 4 Ply* Chilli 666

Needles

Pair each of size 2/3 (3mm) and size 3 (3.25mm) knitting needles
Cable needle

Extras

Stitch markers
6(6:7:7) buttons

Gauge

28 sts and 36 rows to 4in/10cm square over St st using size 3 (3.25mm) needles, *or size to obtain correct gauge*.

Abbreviations

C4B = slip next 2 sts onto cable needle and hold at back of work, k2, then k2 from cable needle.

C4F = slip next 2 sts onto cable needle and hold at front of work, k2, then k2 from cable needle.

Cr2R = slip next st onto cable needle and hold at back of work, k1, then p1 from cable needle.

Cr2L = slip next st onto cable needle and hold at front of work, p1, then k1 from cable needle.

MB = make bobble, [k1, p1, k1] in next st, turn, p3, turn, k3, turn, p3, turn, sl 1, k2tog, psso.

See also page 141.

Note

When working from Charts, right side rows are read from right to left and wrong side rows from left to right.

Back

Using size 2/3 (3mm) needles, cast on 93(99:105:111) sts.

Seed st row K1, [p1, k1] to end.

Rep the last row 7(9:11:13) times.

Change to size 3 (3.25mm) needles.

Row 1 (RS) Seed st 4(7:10:13), work across row 1 of panel A, B, and A, seed st 7, work across row 1 of panel A, B, and A, seed st 4(7:10:13).

Row 2 Seed st 4(7:10:13), work across row 2 of panel A, B, and A, seed st 7, work across row 2 of panel A, B, and A, seed st 4(7:10:13).

These 2 rows set the patt with seed st at sides and in the center.

Work even until back measures 6¼(7:8¼:9¾) in/16(18:21:25)cm from cast-on edge, ending with a wrong side row.

Shape armholes

Bind off 3(4:5:6) sts at beg of next 2 rows.
87(91:95:99) sts.

Work even until back measures 11½(12½:14¼:16¼)in/29(32:36:41)cm from cast-on edge, ending with a wrong side row.

Shape shoulders

Bind off 8 sts at beg of next 4 rows and 8(9:10:11) sts at beg of foll 2 rows.

Bind off rem 39(41:43:45) sts.

Left front

Using size 2/3 (3mm) needles, cast on 53(56:59:62) sts.

Seed st row 1 K1(0:1:0), [p1, k1] to end.

Seed st row 2 [K1, p1] to last 1(0:1:0) st(s), k1(0:1:0).

Rep the last 2 rows 3(4:5:6) times.

Change to size 3 (3.25mm) needles.

Row 1 (RS) Seed st 4(7:10:13), work across row 1 of panel A, B, and A, seed st 10.

Row 2 Seed st 10, work across row 2 of panel A, B, and A, seed st 4(7:10:13).

These 2 rows set the patt with seed st at side and center for front band.

Work even until front measures 6¼(7:8¼:9¾)in/16(18:21:25)cm from cast-on edge, ending with a wrong side row.

Shape armhole

Next row Bind off 3(4:5:6) sts, patt to end.
50(52:54:56) sts.

Work even until front measures 9½(10¾:11¾:13¾)in/24(27:30:35)cm from cast-on edge, ending with a wrong side row.

Shape neck

Next row Patt to last 17(18:19:20) sts, turn and place these sts on a holder.

Dec one st at neck edge on next 9 rows.
24(25:26:27) sts.

Work even until front measures the same as back to shoulder, ending at armhole edge.

Shape shoulder

Bind off 8 sts at beg of next and foll right side row.

Work 1 row.

Bind off rem 8(9:10:11) sts.

Mark position for buttons, the first on the 5th row, the 6th(6th:7th:7th) on the first row of neck shaping, and the rem 4(4:5:5) spaced evenly between.

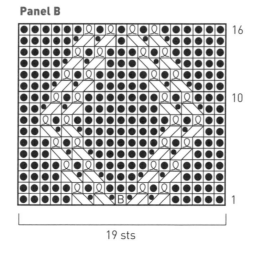

Panel A

8

1

10 sts

Panel B

16

10

1

19 sts

Key

☐ K on RS, P on WS

● P on RS, K on WS

Ω K1tbl on RS, P1tbl on WS

Ⓑ MB

▨ Cr2R

▨ Cr2L

▨ C4B

▨ C4F

Right front

Using size 2/3 (3mm) needles, cast on 53(56:59:62) sts.

Seed st row 1 K1(0:1:0), [p1, k1] to end.

Seed st row 2 [K1, p1] to last 1(0:1:0) st(s), k1(0:1:0).

Rep the last 2 rows once more.

Buttonhole row Seed st 4, work 2tog, yo, seed st to end.

Seed st 3(5:7:9) rows.

Change to size 3 (3.25mm) needles.

Row 1 (RS) Seed st 10, work across row 1 of panel A, B and A, seed st 4(7:10:13).

Row 2 Seed st 4(7:10:13), work across row 2 of panel A, B and A, seed st 10.

These 2 rows set the patt with seed st at side and center for front band.

Working buttonholes to match markers, cont even until front measures 6¼(7:8¼:9¾)in/16(18:21:25)cm from cast-on edge, ending with a right side row.

Shape armhole

Next row Bind off 3(4:5:6) sts, patt to end.
50(52:54:56) sts.

Work even until front measures 9½(10¾:11¾:13¾)in/24(27:30:35)cm from cast-on edge, ending with a wrong side row.

Shape neck

Next row Seed st 4, work 2tog, yo, seed st 4, patt 7(8:9:10) sts, place these 17(18:19:20) sts on a holder, patt to end.

Dec one st at neck edge on next 9 rows.
24(25:26:27) sts.

Work even until front measures the same as back to shoulder shaping, ending at armhole edge.

Shape shoulder

Bind off 8 sts at beg of next and foll wrong side row.

Work 1 row.

Bind off rem 8(9:10:11) sts.

Sleeves

Using size 2/3 (3mm) needles, cast on 45(47:51:55) sts.

Seed st row K1, [p1, k1] to end.

Rep the last row 7(9:11:13) times.

Change to size 3 (3.25mm) needles.

Row 1 (RS) Seed st 3(4:6:8), work across row 1 of panel A, B, and A, seed st 3(4:6:8).

Row 2 Seed st 3(4:6:8), work across row 2 of panel A, B, and A, seed st 3(4:6:8).

These 2 rows set the patt with seed st at sides.

Work 0(4:8:12) rows.

Inc row Seed st 3(4:6:8), m1, patt to last 3(4:6:8) sts, m1, seed st 3(4:6:8).

Work 3 rows.

Rep the last 4 rows 11(13:14:15) times more and the inc row again, working all inc sts into seed st. *71(77:83:89) sts.*

Work even until sleeve measures 6¾(8¼:9¾:11½)in/ 17(21:25:29)cm from cast-on edge, ending with a wrong side row.

Mark each end of last row with a colored thread.

Work 2(4:6:8) rows.

Bind off.

Collar

Join shoulder seams.

With right side facing, using size 2/3 (3mm) needles, slip 17(18:19:20) sts from right front onto a needle, pick up and k20(20:22:22) sts up right side of front neck, 39(41:43:45) sts from back neck, 20(20:22:22) sts down left side of front neck, seed st 17(18:19:20) sts from left front neck holder. *113(117:125:129) sts.*

Work in seed st as set.

Next 2 rows Seed st to last 37(38:41:42) sts, turn.

Next 2 rows Seed st to last 33(33:36:37) sts, turn.

Next 2 rows Seed st to last 29(29:31:32) sts, turn.

Next 2 rows Seed st to last 25(25:26:27) sts, turn.

Next 2 rows Seed st to last 21(21:21:22) sts, turn.

Next 2 rows Seed st to last 17 sts, turn.

Next row Seed st to end.

Work 3 rows.

Bind off 10 sts at beg of next 2 rows. *93(97:105:109) sts.*

Change to size 3 (3.25mm) needles.

Work 20(20:22:22) rows.

Bind off in seed st.

Finishing

Sew in sleeves with rows above colored threads to sts bound off for armhole shaping.

Join side and sleeve seams. Sew on buttons.

bo cardigan

If you love knitting more challenging colorwork, this cardigan is the one to choose. With its fantastic design of little houses and hearts, and its traditional red and white coloring, it is a great modern take on traditional Scandinavian folk knitting. Knitted in *Rowan Fine Tweed*.

Sizes

To fit ages

6–9	12–18	24–36	36–48	months

Actual measurements

Chest

21¾	23¼	25	26¾	in
55	59	64	68	cm

Length to shoulder

12¼	13	15	16½	in
31	33	38	42	cm

Sleeve length

6¾	8¼	9¾	11½	in
17	21	25	29	cm

Yarns

Rowan Fine Tweed
5(5:6:6) x 1oz/98yd balls Bainbridge 369 (A)
4 balls Bell Busk 376 (B)

Needles

Pair each of size 2 (2.75mm) and size 3 (3.25mm) knitting needles

Extras

Stitch holders
7 buttons

Gauge

28 sts and 31 rows to 4in/10cm square over patt on size 3 (3.25mm) needles, *or size to obtain correct gauge.*

Abbreviations

See page 141.

Note

When working from Charts, right side rows are read from right to left and wrong side rows from left to right. Use the Fairisle method and strand yarn across back of work over no more than 3 sts.

Working Back and Sleeves from Chart 1

For the size you are making, take off the center st from the number of sts you have left, divide the remainder by 2, and count this number either side of the center st, this will be your starting and finishing point.

Back

Using size 2 (2.75mm) needles and A, cast on 79(85:91:97) sts.
Rib row 1 K1, [p1, k1] to end.
Rib row 2 P1, [k1, p1] to end.
Rep the last 2 rows 5(6:6:7) times more.
Change to size 3 (3.25mm) needles.
Work in St st and patt from Chart 1.

1st size only

Beg at row 1 work to end of row 40.

2nd size only

Beg at row 37, work to end of row 40, then beg at row 1, work to end of row 40.

3rd size only

Beg at row 1, work to end of row 40, then work from row 1–14.

4th size only

Beg at row 37, work to end of row 40, then beg at row 1, work to end of row 40, then work from row 1–20.

All sizes

Row 1 Using B, knit to end.
Row 2 Using A, purl to end.
Row 3 K6(9:12:15)B, work across row 3 of Chart 2, k6(9:12:15)B.
Row 4 P6(9:12:15)B, work across row 4 of Chart 2, p6(9:12:15)B.
These 2 rows set the patt.
Cont in patt to end of row 31.
Cont in B only.
Work 11(13:17:19) rows.

Shape upper arms

Bind off 4 sts at beg of next 2 rows and 4(5:6:7) sts at beg of foll 2 rows. *63(67:71:75) sts.*
Bind off 7(8:8:9) sts at beg of next 2 rows and 8(8:9:9)

Chart 1

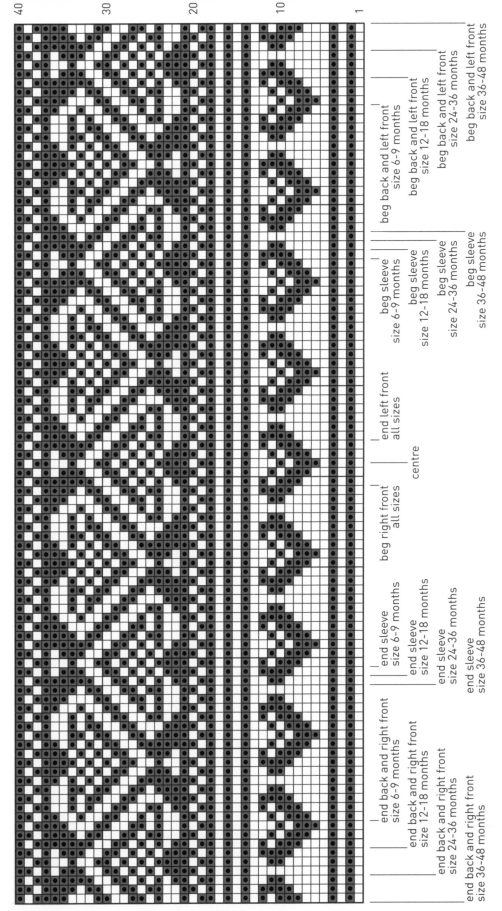

Key

● Bainbridge (A)

☐ Bell Busk (B)

Chart 2

Right Front (32 sts)

Left Front (37 sts)

Back (67 sts)

Key

■ Bainbridge (A)

□ Bell Busk (B)

sts at beg of foll 2 rows.
Leave rem 33(35:37:39) sts on a holder.

Left front

Using size 2 (2.75mm) needles and A, cast on
37(39:43:45) sts.
Rib row 1 P1, [k1, p1] to end.
Rib row 2 K1, [p1, k1] to end.
Rep the last 2 rows 5(6:6:7) times more, inc one st at
center of row on 2nd and 4th sizes only.
37(40:43:46) sts.
Change to size 3 (3.25mm) needles.
Work in St st and patt from Chart 1.

1st size only
Beg at row 1, work to end of row 40.

2nd size only
Beg at row 37, work to end of row 40, then beg at row 1
work to end of row 40.

3rd size only
Beg at row 1, work to end of row 40, then work from
row 1–14.

4th size only
Beg at row 37, work to end of row 40, then beg at row 1
work to end of row 40, then work from row 1–20.

All sizes
Row 1 Using B, knit to end.

Row 2 Using A, purl to end.

Row 3 K0(2:4:6)B, work first 37 sts of row 3 of Chart 2, k0(1:2:3)B.

Row 4 P0(1:2:3)B, work last 37 sts of row 4 of Chart 2, p0(2:4:6)B.

These 2 rows set the patt.

Cont in patt to end of row 31, then cont in B only **at the same time** when row 26 of chart has been worked, ending with a wrong side row.

Shape front neck

Next row Patt to last 6(7:8:9) sts, turn and leave these sts on a holder.

Dec one st at neck edge on every row until 23(25:27:29) sts rem.

Work even until front measures the same as back to upper arm, ending at side edge.

Shape upper arm

Bind off 4 sts at beg of next row and 4(5:6:7) sts at beg of foll right side row. *15(16:17:18) sts.*

Shape shoulder

Work 1 row.

Bind off 7(8:8:9) sts at beg of next row.

Work 1 row.

Bind off rem 8(8:9:9) sts.

Right front

Using size 2 (2.75mm) needles and A, cast on 37(39:43:45) sts.

Rib row 1 P1, [k1, p1] to end.

Rib row 2 K1, [p1, k1] to end.

Rep the last 2 rows 5(6:6:7) times more, inc one st at center of row on 2nd and 4th sizes only. *37(40:43:46) sts.*

Change to size 3 (3.25mm) needles.

Work in St st and patt from Chart 1.

1st size only

Beg at row 1 work to end of row 40.

2nd size only

Beg at row 37, work to end of row 40, then beg at row 1, work to end of row 40.

3rd size only

Beg at row 1 work to end of row 40, then work from row 1–14.

4th size only

Beg at row 37, work to end of row 40, then beg at row 1, work to end of row 40, then work from row 1–20.

All sizes

Row 1 Using B, knit to end.

Row 2 Using A, purl to end.

Row 3 K3(4:5:6)B, work last 32 sts of row 3 of Chart 2, k2(4:6:8)B.

Row 4 P2(4:6:8)B, work first 32 sts of row 4 of Chart 2, p3(4:5:6)B.

These 2 rows set the patt.

Cont in patt to end of row 31, then cont in B only **at the same time** when row 26 of Chart has been worked, end with a wrong side row.

Shape front neck

Next row Patt 6(7:8:9) sts, leave these sts on a holder, patt to end.

Dec one st at neck edge on every row until 23(25:27:29) sts rem.

Work even until front measures the same as back to upper arm shaping, ending at side edge.

Shape upper arm

Bind off 4 sts at beg of next row and 4(5:6:7) sts at beg of foll wrong side row. *15(16:17:18) sts.*

Shape shoulder

Work 1 row.

Bind off 7(8:8:9) sts at beg of next row.

Work 1 row.

Bind off rem 8(8:9:9) sts.

Sleeves

Patt rows for sleeves

1st size only

Beg at row 1, work to end of row 40.

2nd size only

Beg at row 1, work to end of row 40, then work rows 1–14 again.

3rd size only

Beg at row 37, work to end of row 40, then work rows 1 to 40, then work from row 1–20.

4th size only

Beg at row 17, work to end of row 40, then beg at row 1 work to end of row 40, then work from row 1–14.

Using size 2 (2.75mm) needles and A, cast on 47(49:58:55) sts.

Rib row 1 K1, [p1, k1] to end.

Rib row 2 P1, [k1, p1] to end.

Rep the last 2 rows 5(5:6:6) times more.

Change to size 3 (3.25mm) needles.

Work in St st and patt from Chart, at the same time, inc one st at each end of the 3rd and 9(11:13:16) foll 4th rows. 67(73:81:89) sts.

Work even until all the rows have been worked.

Bind off.

Neckband

Join shoulder seams.

With right side facing, using size 2 (2.75mm) needles and B, place 6(7:8:9) sts from right front holder on needle, pick up and k19(21:23:25) sts up right side of front neck, k33(35:37:39) sts from back neck, pick up and k19(21:23:25) sts down left side of front neck, k6(7:8:9) from left front holder. 83(91:99:107) sts.

Rib row 1 K1, [p1,k1] to end.

Rib row 2 P1, [k1, p1] to end.

Rep the last 2 rows twice more.

Break off B, join on A.

Work 1 row.

Bind off in rib.

Buttonband

With right side facing, using size 2 (2.75mm) needles and A, pick up and k66(72:80:87) sts evenly down front edge of left front.

Knit 4 rows.

Bind off.

Buttonhole band

With right side facing, using size 2 (2.75mm) needles and A, pick up and k68(72:80:87) sts evenly up front edge of right front.

Knit 1 row.

Buttonhole row K1(1:2:2), [k2tog, y2o, skpo, k6(7:8:9)] 6 times, k2tog, y2o, skpo, k1(1:2:3).

Knit 2 rows.

Bind off.

Finishing

Sew on sleeves, placing center of cast-off row to shoulder seam. Join side and sleeve seams. Sew on buttons.

folk bag

A cute, small tote bag featuring little Scandinavian people, this would make a lovely present for a small girl. Knitted in Rowan *Felted Tweed DK*.

Size

Approx 8in/20cm wide by 8in/20cm deep

Yarns

Rowan *Felted Tweed DK*
2 x 1¾oz/191yd balls Clay 177 (A)
One ball each Seafarer 170 (B), Avocado 161 (C), and Rage 150 (D)

Needles

Pair each of size 3 (3.25mm) and size 5 (3.75mm) knitting needles

Extras

Lining fabric 9¾ x 35½in/25 x 90cm
27½in/70cm of 1-in/2.5-cm wide petersham ribbon
Cardboard

Gauge

26 sts and 26 rows to 4in/10cm square over patt using size 5 (3.75mm) needles, *or size to obtain correct gauge.*

Abbreviations

See page 141.

Note

When working from Chart, right side rows are read from right to left and wrong side rows from left to right. Use the Fairisle method, strand the yarn not in use across the wrong side of work weaving them under and over the working yarn every 3 or 4 sts.

Front

Using size 5 (3.75mm) needles and A, cast on 54 sts.
Beg with a knit row, work in St st and patt from chart, working rows 1–46.
Change to size 3 (3.25mm) needles.
Knit 7 rows.
Bind off knitwise.

Back

Using size 5 (3.75mm) needles and A, cast on 54 sts.
Beg with a knit row, work in St st and patt from chart working rows 24–46, then rows 1–23.
Change to size 3 (3.25mm) needles.
Knit 7 rows.
Bind off knitwise.

Left gusset

Using size 5 (3.75mm) needles and A, cast on 15 sts.
Beg with a knit row, work 28 rows in St st.
Now work in patt from chart working rows 1–46.
Change to size 3 (3.25mm) needles.
Knit 7 rows.
Bind off knitwise.

Right gusset

Using size 5 (3.75mm) needles and A, cast on 15 sts.
Beg with a knit row, work 28 rows in St st.
Now work in patt from chart working rows 24–46, then rows 1–23.
Change to size 3 (3.25mm) needles.
Knit 7 rows.
Bind off knitwise.

Handles (make 2)

Using size 5 (3.75mm) needles and A, cast on 17 sts.

Next row K4, sl 1pw, k7, sl 1pw, k4.

Next row Purl to end.

Rep the last 2 rows 43 times more.

Bind off.

Finishing

Using knitted pieces as a template and adding seam allowance, cut out front, back, and side gusset pieces from lining.

Join cast-on edges of gussets.

Sew row ends of gusset to row ends and cast-on edges of back and front. Make up lining in same way. Place lining inside bag, fold seam allowance to wrong side, and slip stitch lining in place.

Cut petersham ribbon in half. Place petersham ribbon along center of wrong side of handle and slip stitch in place along slipped sts. Bring row ends of handle together encasing petersham ribbon and sew row ends together. For extra stiffness in bottom of bag, cut a piece of cardboard to fit bottom. From lining make a "bag" to fit cardboard. Place in bottom of bag.

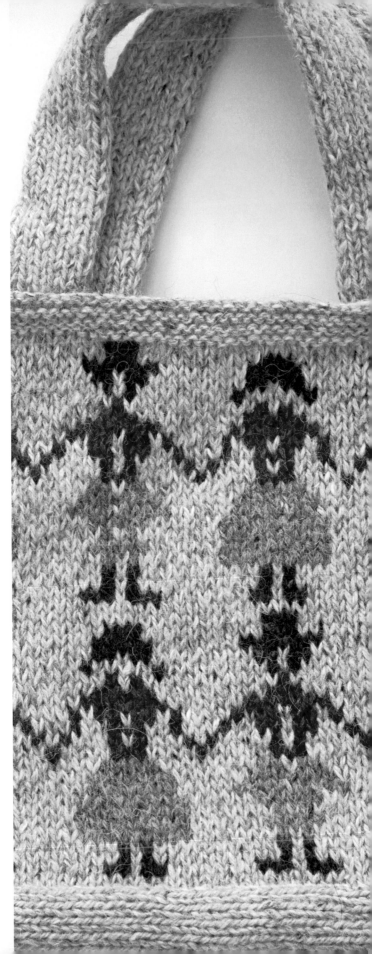

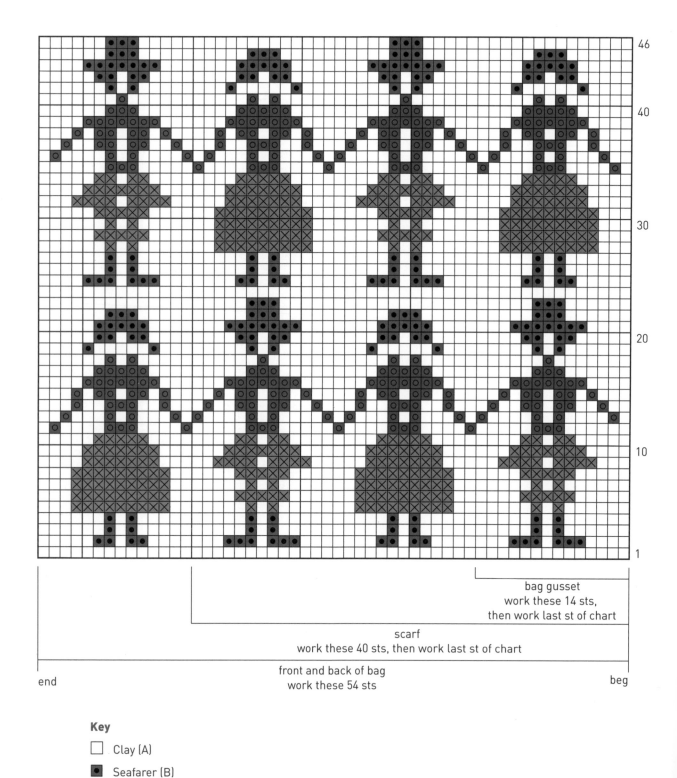

46

40

30

20

10

1

bag gusset
work these 14 sts,
then work last st of chart

scarf
work these 40 sts, then work last st of chart

front and back of bag
work these 54 sts

end

beg

Key

☐ Clay (A)

⬛ Seafarer (B)

☒ Avocado (C)

⬛ Rage (D)

folk scarf

And here is the scarf to accompany the bag! Knitted in simple stripes it has the little Scandinavian people featured on the pockets at each end. Also knitted in Rowan *Felted Tweed DK*.

Size

Approx 6in/15cm wide by 56in/142cm long

Yarns

Rowan *Felted Tweed DK*
2 x 1¾oz/191yd balls Clay 177 (A)
One ball each Seafarer 170 (B), Avocado 161 (C), and
Rage 150 (D)

Needles

Pair each of size 3 (3.25mm) and size 5 (3.75mm)
knitting needles

Gauge

26 sts and 26 rows to 4in/10cm square over patt using
size 5 (3.75mm) needles, *or size to obtain correct gauge.*

Abbreviations

See page 141.

Note

When working from Chart, right side rows are read
from right to left and wrong side rows from left to
right. Use the Fairisle method, strand the yarn not
in use across the wrong side of work weaving them
under and over the working yarn every 3 or 4 sts.

Pocket (make 2)

Using size 5 (3.75mm) needles and A, cast on 41 sts.
Beg with a knit row, work in St st and patt from chart
working rows 1–46.
Change to size 3 (3.25mm) needles.
Cont in A only.
Row 47 K20, k2tog, k19. *40 sts.*
Row 48 P3, [k2, p2] to last 5 sts, k2, p3.
Row 48 Knit to end.
Rep the last 2 rows once more.
Bind off.

Scarf

Using size 5 (3.75mm) needles and A, cast on 80 sts.
Beg with a knit row, work in St st and stripes of 4
rows A, 4 rows D, 4 rows B, and 4 rows C until scarf
measures 55½in/141cm, ending 4 rows A.
Bind off.

Finishing

With cast-on edges of pockets level with cast-on and
bound-off edges of scarf, sew one pocket centrally to
each end of scarf.
Join row ends of scarf together.
With seam running down center of back, using size
3 (3.25mm) needles and D, working through both
thicknesses, pick up and k40 sts along one short end.
Knit 2 rows.
Bind off.
Work other end to match.

norse hat

And now one for the boys! A lovely beanie knitted in the traditional bird's-eye design with a contrasting colored rib. Knitted in Rowan *Felted Tweed DK*.

Sizes

To fit 6–18 (24–48) months.
Circumference 16¾(18¾)in/42.5(47.5)cm

Yarns

One 1¾oz/191yd ball each of Rowan *Felted Tweed DK* in Scree 165 (A), Seafarer 170 (B), Maritime 167 (C), and Ginger 154 (D)

Needles

Pair each of size 3 (3.25mm) and size 5 (3.75mm) knitting needles

Gauge

23 sts and 28 rows to 4in/10cm square over patt using size 5 (3.75mm) needles, *or size to obtain correct gauge.*

Abbreviations

See page 141.

To make

Using size 3 (3.25mm) needles and D, cast on 98(110) sts.
Row 1 P2, [k2, p2] to end.
Row 2 K2, [p2, k2] to end.
These 2 rows form the rib.
Work a further 8 rows.
Change to size 5 (3.75mm) needles.
Beg with a knit row, work in St st.
Row 1 Using B, work to end.
Row 2 Using B, work to end.
Row 3 Work 2B, [1A, 2B] to end.
Row 4 Using B, work to end.
Row 5 Using B, work to end.
Row 6 Using C, work to end.
Row 7 Using C, work to end.
Row 8 Work 2C, [1B, 2C] to end.
Row 9 Using C, work to end.
Row 10 Using C, work to end.

Row 11 Using A, work to end.
Row 12 Using A, work to end.
Row 13 Work 2A, [1C, 2A] to end.
Row 14 Using A, work to end.
Row 15 Using A, work to end.
These 15 rows form the stripe patt.
Work a further 15 rows.

Crown

Using B, beg with a knit row cont in St st only.
Work 2(6) rows, inc 3(1) st(s) evenly across last row. *101(111) sts.*

Shaping

Row 1 [K8(9), k2tog] 10 times, k1. *91(101) sts.*
Row 2 Purl to end.
Row 3 [K7(8), k2tog] 10 times, k1. *81(91) sts.*
Row 4 Purl to end.
Row 5 [K6(7), k2tog] 10 times, k1. *71(81) sts.*
Row 6 Purl to end.
Row 7 [K5(6), k2tog] 10 times, k1. *61(71) sts.*
Row 8 Purl to end.
Row 9 [K4(5), k2tog] 10 times, k1. *51(61) sts.*
Row 10 Purl to end.
Row 11 [K3(4), k2tog] 10 times, k1. *41(51) sts.*
Row 12 Purl to end.
Row 13 [K2(3), k2tog] 10 times, k1. *31(41) sts.*
Row 14 Purl to end.
Row 15 [K1(2), k2tog] 10 times, k1. *21(31) sts.*

2nd size only

Row 16 Purl to end.
Row 17 [K-(1), k2tog] 10 times, k1. *21 sts.*

Both sizes

Next row Purl to end.
Next row [K2tog] 10 times, k1. *11 sts.*
Next row Purl to end.
Break off yarn, thread through rem sts, and fasten off.

Finishing

Join seam.

norse scarf

The accompanying scarf to the hat, with matching contrast-colored ribbed ends. Also knitted in Rowan *Felted Tweed DK*.

Size

5(5½:6:6¼)in/13(14:15:16)cm wide by
41¾(45½:49½:53½)in/106(116:126:136)cm long

Yarns

Rowan *Felted Tweed DK*
2 x 1¾oz/191yd balls each Scree 165 (A), Seafarer 170 (B), and Maritime 167 (C)
One ball Ginger 154 (D)

Needles

Pair each of size 3 (3.25mm) and size 5 (3.75mm) knitting needles

Gauge

23 sts and 28 rows to 4in/10cm square over patt using size 5 (3.75mm) needles, *or size to obtain correct gauge.*

Abbreviations

See page 141.

To make

Using size 5 (3.75mm) needles and B, cast on 59(65:71:77) sts.
Beg with a knit row, work in St st.
Row 1 Using B, work to end.
Row 2 Using B, work to end.
Row 3 Work 2B, [1A, 2B] to end.
Row 4 Using B,work to end.
Row 5 Using B, work to end.
Row 6 Using C, work to end.
Row 7 Using C, work to end.

Row 8 Work 2C, [1B, 2C] to end.
Row 9 Using C, work to end.
Row 10 Using C, work to end.
Row 11 Using A, work to end.
Row 12 Using A, work to end.
Row 13 Work 2A, [1C, 2A] to end.
Row 14 Using A, work to end.
Row 15 Using A, work to end.
These 15 rows form the stripe patt.
Cont in patt until scarf measures 39½(43¼:47¼:51)in/ 100(110:120:130)cm, ending row 5.
Using B, bind off.

Finishing

Join row ends together.
With seam running down center of back, using size 3 (3.25mm) needles and D, working through both thicknesses, pick up and k30(34:34:38) sts along one short end.
Row 1 P2, [k2, p2] to end.
Row 2 K2, [p2, k2] to end.
These 2 rows form the rib.
Work a further 7 rows.
Bind off in rib.
Work other end to match.

lara sweater

This little cable and checkerboard pattern makes a sweet split-necked sweater for little girls. Knitted in Rowan *Cotton Glacé*, the stitch detail shows up beautifully.

Sizes

To fit ages

6–9	12–18	24–36	36–48	months

Actual measurements

Chest

20½	22¾	25½	28¼	in
52	58	65	72	cm

Length to shoulder

10¾	11¾	13¼	15¼	in
27	30	34	39	cm

Sleeve length

6¾	8¼	9¾	11½	in
17	21	25	29	cm

Yarn

4(5:5:6) x 1¾oz/125yd balls of Rowan *Cotton Glacé* Sky 749

Needles

Pair each of size 2/3 (3mm) and size 3 (3.25mm) knitting needles
Cable needle

Extras

Stitch holders
3 buttons

Gauge

30 sts and 40 rows to 4in/10cm square over patt using size 3 (3.25mm) needles, *or size to obtain correct gauge.*

Abbreviations

C4B = slip next 2 sts onto cable needle and hold at back of work, k2, then k2 from cable needle.
C4F = slip next 2 sts onto cable needle and hold at front of work, k2, then k2 from cable needle.
See also page 141.

Note

When working from Chart, right side rows are read from right to left and wrong side rows from left to right. When there are not enough sts to work a cable, work these sts in St st.

Back

Using size 2/3 (3mm) needles, cast on 80(90:100:110) sts.
Rib row [K1, p1] to end.
Rep the last row 11(13:13:15) times more.
Change to size 3 (3.25mm) needles.
Row 1 (RS) Work last 3 sts of patt rep, [work across row 1 of patt rep] 7(8:9:10) times, work first 7 sts of patt rep.
Row 2 Work last 7 sts of patt rep, [work across row 2 of patt rep] 7(8:9:10) times, work first 3 sts of patt rep.
These 2 rows set the patt.
Cont in patt until back measures 6(6¾:7¾:9½)in/ 15(17:20:24)cm from cast-on edge, ending with a wrong side row.
Shape armholes
Bind off 8 sts at beg of next 2 rows. *64(74:84:94) sts.*
Work even until back measures 10½(11¾:13¼:15¼)in/ 27(30:34:39)cm from cast-on edge, ending with a wrong side row.
Shape shoulders
Bind off 5(6:8:9) sts at beg of next 4 rows and 5(7:7:9) sts at beg of foll 2 rows.
Leave rem 34(36:38:40) sts on a holder.

Pocket linings (make 2)

Using size 2/3 (3mm) needles, cast on 16 sts.
Beg with a knit row, work 13(19:25:31) rows in St st.
Inc row P4, [m1, p3] 4 times. *20 sts.*
Leave these sts on a holder.

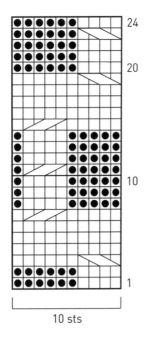

24

20

10

1

10 sts

Key

☐ K on RS, P on WS

▣ P on RS, K on WS

▨ C4B

▧ C4F

Front

Work as given for back until 14(20:26:32) rows have been worked in patt.

Place pocket

Next row Patt 12(14:16:18), place next 20 sts on a holder, patt across 20 sts of first pocket lining, patt 16(22:28:34), place next 20 sts on a holder, patt across 20 sts of second pocket lining, patt 12(14:16:18).

Cont in patt until front measures 6(6¾:7¾:9½)in/15(17:20:24)cm from cast-on edge, ending with a wrong side row.

Shape armholes

Bind off 8 sts at beg of next 2 rows. *64(74:84:94) sts.*

Divide for front opening

Next row Patt 29(34:39:44), turn, and work on these sts for first side of front.

Work even until front measures 9(10¼:11¾:13¾)in/23(26:30:35)cm from cast-on edge, ending with a wrong side row.

Shape front neck

Next row Patt to last 7(8:9:10) sts, leave these sts on a holder, turn.

Dec one st at neck edge on every row until 15(19:23:27) sts rem.

Work even until front measures the same as back to shoulder, ending at armhole edge.

Shape shoulder

Bind off 5(6:8:9) sts at beg of next and foll right side row.

Work 1 row.

Bind off rem sts.

With right side facing, slip center 6 sts on a holder, rejoin yarn to next st, patt to end.

Work even until front measures 9(10¼:11¾:13¾)in/23(26:30:35)cm from cast-on edge, ending with a wrong side row.

Shape front neck

Next row Patt 7(8:9:10) sts, leave these sts on a holder, patt to end.

Dec one st at neck edge on every row until 15(19:23:27) sts rem.

Work even until front measures the same as back to shoulder, ending at armhole edge.

Shape shoulder

Bind off 5(6:8:9) sts at beg of next and foll wrong side row.

Work 1 row.

Bind off rem sts.

Sleeves

Using size 2/3 (3mm) needles, cast on 40(44:48:52) sts.

Rib row [K1, p1] to end.

Rep the last row 11(13:13:15) times more.

Change to size 3 (3.25mm) needles.

Row 1 (RS) Work 3(5:2:4) sts of patt rep, [work across row 1 of patt rep] 3(3:4:4) times, work first 7(9:6:8) sts of patt rep.

Row 2 Work last 7(9:6:8) sts of patt rep, [work across row 2 of patt rep] 3(3:4:4) times, work first 3(5:2:4) sts of patt rep.

These 2 rows set the patt.

Inc and work into patt, one st at each end of the next and every foll 4th row until there are 66(74:82:88) sts.

Work even until sleeve measures 6¾(8¼:9¾:11½)in/17(21:25:29)cm from cast-on edge, ending with a wrong side row.

Mark each end of last row with a colored thread.

Work 10 rows.

Bind off.

Buttonband

Using size 2/3 (3mm) needles, cast on 9 sts.

Rib row 1 K2, p1, [k1, p1] twice, k2.

Rib row 2 [K1, p1] to last st, k1.

Rep the last 2 rows 14(16:18:20) times, leave these sts on a holder.

Buttonhole band

With right side facing, using size 2/3 (3mm) needles, work across sts at center front as foll: k1, m1, k2, m1, k2, m1, k1. *9 sts.*

Rib row 1 [K1, p1] to last st, k1.

Rib row 2 K2, p1, [k1, p1] twice, k2.

Rep last 2 rows twice more and the first row again.

Buttonhole row Rib 4, yo, k2tog, rib 3.

Rib 11(13:15:17) rows.

Buttonhole row Rib 4, yo, k2tog, rib 3.

Rib 9(11:13:15) rows.

Do not fasten off.

Neckband

Join shoulder seams.

With right side facing, using size 2/3 (3mm) needles, rib 8 from buttonhole band, purl next st tog with first st on right front holder, k6(7:8:9), pick up and k17 sts up right side of front neck, k34(36:38:40) from back neck, pick up and k18 sts down left side of front neck, then purl next st tog with first st on buttonband, rib 8.

Next row Rib to end.

Buttonhole row Rib 4, yo, k2tog, rib to end.

Rib 3 rows.

Bind off in rib.

Finishing

Sew in sleeves with last 10 rows to bound-off sts. Join side and sleeve seams. Sew buttonband and buttonhole bands in place. Sew buttonband to back of buttonhole band. Sew on buttons.

finn sweater

This easy-to-wear sweater with a loose, slightly rolled neck is very comfortable. It features lovely textured stitches and a twisted cable design. Knitted in Rowan *Wool Cotton*.

Sizes

To fit ages

6–9	12–18	24–36	36–48	months

Actual measurements

Chest

20½	23¼	26	28¾	in
52	59	66	73	cm

Length to shoulder

10¾	11¾	13½	15¼	in
27	30	34	39	cm

Sleeve length

6¾	8¼	9¾	11½	in
17	21	25	29	cm

Yarns

6(6:7:7) x 1¾oz/123yd balls of Rowan *Wool Cotton* Clear 941

Needles

Pair each of size 5 (3.75mm) and size 6 (4mm) knitting needles
Cable needle

Gauge

22 sts and 30 rows to 4in/10cm square over St st using size 6 (4mm) needles.
25 sts sts and 36 rows to 4in/10cm square over patt using size 6 (4mm) needles.
Or size to obtain correct gauge.

Abbreviations

C6B = slip next 3 sts onto cable needle and hold at back of work, k3, then k3 from cable needle.
See also page 141.

Back

Using size 5 (3.75mm) needles, cast on 70(78:86:94) sts.

Row 1 (RS) [K2, p2] 3(4:5:6) times, * k6, p2, [k2, p2] 3 times; rep from * once more, k6, [p2, k2] 3(4:5:6) times.

Row 2 [P2, k2] 3(4:5:6) times, * p6, k2, [p2, k2] 3 times; rep from * once more, p6, [k2, p2] 3(4:5:6) times.

Row 3 [K2, p2] 3(4:5:6) times, * C6B, p2, [k2, p2] 3 times; rep from * once more, C6B, [p2, k2] 3(4:5:6) times.

Row 4 [P2, k2] 3(4:5:6) times, * p6, k2, [p2, k2] 3 times; rep from * once more, p6, [k2, p2] 3(4:5:6) times.

Rows 5–10(10:14:14) Rep rows 1– 4 1(1:2:2) time(s), then rows 1 and 2 again.

Change to size 6 (4mm) needles.

Row 1 [K1, p1] 4(6:8:10) times, * k2, p2, C6B, p2, k2, [p1, k1] 3 times; rep from * once more, k2, p2, C6B, p2, k2, [p1, k1] 4(6:8:10) times.

Row 2 [K1, p1] 4(6:8:10) times, * p2, k2, p6, k2, p2, [k1, p1] 3 times; rep from * once more, p2, k2, p6, k2, p2, [p1, k1] 4(6:8:10) times.

Row 3 [K1, p1] 4(6:8:10) times, * k2, p2, k6, p2, k2, [p1, k1] 3 times; rep from * once more, k2, p2, k6, p2, k2, [p1, k1] 4(6:8:10) times.

Row 4 [K1, p1] 4(6:8:10) times, * p2, k2, p6, k2, p2, [k1, p1] 3 times; rep from * once more, p2, k2, p6, k2, p2, [p1, k1] 4(6:8:10) times.

These 4 rows form the patt.

Cont in patt until back measures 5½(6¼:7½:9)in/ 14(16:19:23)cm from cast-on edge, ending with a wrong side row.

Shape armholes

Bind off 4(5:6:7) sts at beg of next 2 rows. *62(68:74:80) sts.*

Work even until back measures 10¾(11¾:13½:15¼)in/ 27(30:34:39)cm from cast-on edge, ending with a wrong side row.

Shape shoulders

Bind off 5(6:7:8) sts at beg of next 4 rows and 5 sts at beg of foll 2 rows.

Leave rem 32(34:36:38) sts on a holder.

Front

Work as given for back until front measures 9(10¼:11¾:13¾)in/23(26:30:35)cm from cast-on edge, ending with a wrong side row.

Divide for neck

Row 1 Patt 21(23:25:27), turn, and work on these sts.

Dec one st at neck edge on next 6 rows. *15(17:19:21) sts.*

Work even until front measures the same as back to shoulder, ending at armhole edge.

Shape shoulder

Next row Bind off 5(6:7:8) sts at beg of next and foll right side row.

Work 1 row.

Bind off rem sts.

With right side facing, place center 20(22:24:26) sts on a holder, rejoin yarn to rem sts, patt to end. *21(23:25:27) sts.*

Dec one st at neck edge on next 6 rows. *15(17:19:21) sts.*

Work even until front measures the same as back to shoulder, ending at armhole edge.

Shape shoulder

Next row Bind off 5(6:7:8) sts at beg of next and foll wrong side row.

Work 1 row.

Bind off rem sts.

Sleeves

Using size 5 (3.75mm) needles, cast on 34(34:42:42) sts.

Row 1 (RS) [K2, p2] 1(1:2:2) time(s), k6, p2, [k2, p2] 3 times, k6, [p2, k2] 1(1:2:2) time(s).

Row 2 [P2, k2] 1(1:2:2) time(s), p6, k2, [p2, k2] 3 times, p6, [k2, p2] 1(1:2:2) time(s).

Row 3 [K2, p2] 1(1:2:2) time(s), C6B, p2, [k2, p2] 3 times, C6B, [p2, k2] 1(1:2:2) time(s).

Row 4 [P2, k2] 1(1:2:2) time(s), p6, k2, [p2, k2] 3 times, p6, [k2, p2] 1(1:2:2) time(s).

Rows 5–10(10:14:14) Rep rows 1–4 1(1:2:2) time(s), then rows 1 and 2 again.

Change to size 6 (4mm) needles.

Row 1 [K1, p1] 0(0:2:2) times, k2, p2, C6B, p2, k2, [p1, k1] 3 times, k2, p2, C6B, p2, k2, [p1, k1] 0(0:2:2) times.

Row 2 [K1, p1] 0(0:2:2) times, p2, k2, p6, k2, p2, [k1, p1] 3 times, p2, k2, p6, k2, p2, [p1, k1] 0(0:2:2) times.

Row 3 [K1, p1] 0(0:2:2) times, k2, p2, k6, p2, k2, [p1, k1] 3 times, k2, p2, k6, p2, k2, [p1, k1] 0(0:2:2) times.

Row 4 [K1, p1] 0(0:2:2) times, p2, k2, p6, k2, p2, [k1, p1] 3 times, p2, k2, p6, k2, p2, [p1, k1] 0(0:2:2) times.

Inc and work into seed st, one st at each end of the next and every foll 4th row until there are 54(60:70:76) sts.

Work even until sleeve measures 6¾(8¼:9¾:11½)in/ 17(21:25:29)cm from cast-on edge, ending with a wrong side row.

Mark each end of last row with a colored thread.

Work a further 6(8:8:10) rows.

Bind off.

Neckband

Join right shoulder seam.

With right side facing, using size 5 (3.75mm) needles, pick up and k15 sts down left side of front neck, k20(22:24:26) from center front neck holder, pick up and k15 sts up right side of front neck, k32(34:36:38) from back neck holder. *82(86:90:94) sts.*

Row 1 P2, [k2, p2] to end.

Row 2 K2, [p2, k2] to end.

Rep the last 2 rows twice more and the first row again.

Starting with a knit row, work 6 rows St st.

Bind off.

Finishing

Join left shoulder and neckband.

Sew in sleeves with last 6(8:8:10) rows to bound-off sts. Join side and sleeve seams.

tundra cushion

A lovely little cushion for the nursery with its pattern of differently shaped trees is knitted in Rowan *Felted Tweed DK*, making it beautifully soft. A treat for anyone who enjoys colorwork knitting!

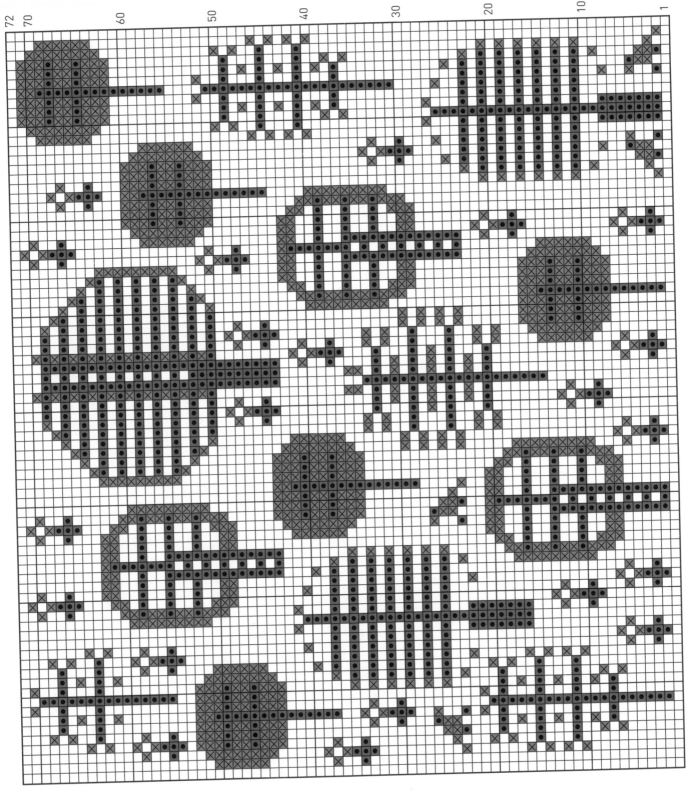

Key

Clay (A)

Pine (B)

Avocado (C)

Size

11¾ x 11¾in/30 x 30cm

Yarns

One 1¾oz/191yd ball each of Rowan *Felted Tweed DK*
Clay 177 (A), Pine 158 (B), and Avocado 161 (C)

Needles

Pair each of size 5 (3.75mm) and size 6 (4mm) knitting
needles

Extras

10in/25cm zipper
Cushion form

Gauge

22 sts and 28 rows to 4in/10cm square over St st using
size 6 (4mm) needles.
26 sts and 24 rows to 4in/10cm square over St st and
patt using size 5 (3.75mm) needles.
Or size to obtain correct gauge.

Abbreviations

See page 141.

Note

When working from Chart, right side rows are read
from right to left and wrong side rows from left to
right.

Front

Using size 5 (3.75mm) needles and A, cast on 79 sts.
Using a combination of Fairisle and intarsia, beg with
a knit row, work in St st, and patt from chart to end of
row 72.
Using A, bind off.

Back

Lower back

Using size 6 (4mm) needles and A, cast on 66 sts.
Beg with a knit row, work 60 rows in St st and stripes
of 4 rows A, 4 rows B, and 4 rows C.
Using C, bind off.

Upper back

Using size 6 (4mm) needles and A, cast on 66 sts.
Beg with a knit row, work 24 rows in St st and stripes
of 4 rows A, 4 rows B, and 4 rows C.
Using C, bind off.

Finishing

Leaving 10in/25cm opening for zipper, sew upper back
to lower back. Sew in zipper. With right sides together,
sew back to front. Turn to right side.
Insert cushion form.

pattern information

Sizing

The instructions in the patterns are given for the smallest size first, and larger sizes follow in parentheses. If there is only one set of figures, it refers to all sizes. If - (hyphen) or 0 (zero) is given in an instruction for the size you are knitting, then that particular instruction does not apply to your size.

Gauge

The correct gauge can make the difference between a successful garment and a disastrous one. It controls both the shape and size of an article, so any variation, however slight, can distort the finished garment.

You must match the gauge given at the start of each pattern. To check your gauge, knit a square in the pattern stitch and/or stockinette stitch of perhaps 5–10 more stitches and 5–10 more rows than those given in the gauge note. Press the finished square under a damp cloth and mark out the central 4in/10cm square with pins. If you have too many stitches to 4in/10cm, try again using thicker needles. If you have too few stitches to 4in/10cm, try again using finer needles. Once you have achieved the correct gauge, your garment will be knitted to the right size.

Cable patterns

Cable stitch patterns allow you to twist the stitches in various ways, to create decorative effects such as an interesting rope-like structure to the knitting. The cables can be thin and fine (just a couple of stitches wide) or really big and chunky (up to 8 stitches or more).

To work cables, you need to hold the appropriate number of stitches that form the cable twist (abbreviated in pattern as C) on a separate small cable needle, while you knit behind or in front of them. You then knit the stitches off the cable needle before continuing to knit the remaining stitches in the row.

Depending on whether the cable needle is at the front or the back of the work, the cables will twist to the left or right but the principle remains the same. A four-stitch cable will be abbreviated as C4F or C4B depending on whether the cable needle is held to the front or back of the work.

Colorwork knitting

There are two main methods of working with color in knitted fabrics: the intarsia and the Fairisle techniques. The first method produces a single thickness of fabric and is usually used where a new color is required for a block of stitches and rows in a particular area of a piece of knitting. Where a small repeating color pattern of up to 3 or 4 stitches is created across the row, the Fairisle technique is generally used.

Intarsia

For this technique, you join in a new yarn color for each new block of color stitches. To prevent the yarns getting twisted on the ball, the simplest method is to make individual little balls of yarn, or bobbins, from pre-cut short lengths of yarn, one for each motif or block of color used in a row. You then work across the stitches, joining in the colors as required, by twisting them around each other where they meet on the wrong side of the work, to avoid gaps. After you have completed the piece of knitting, you need to neaten the loose ends. They can either be darned along the color joins, or they can be knitted in to the fabric as each color is worked by picking up the loops of the yarns carried across the back of the work as you knit.

Fairisle

When you are working a pattern with two or more repeating colors in the same row, you need to strand the yarn not in use behind the stitches being worked.

This needs to be done with care, loosely enough to ensure that the strands not in work do not tighten and pucker the front of the knitting. To do this, treat the yarns not in use (known as "floating yarns") as if they were one yarn and spread the stitches as you work to their correct width to keep them elastic. If your pattern demands that the stranded or floating yarns are carried across more than three stitches, it is wise to weave the new yarn color under and over the color yarn you are working with each time you change colors (over the first time, under the second time, and so on). The alternating "under and over" movement helps to prevent the floating yarns from tangling by keeping them caught at the back of the work.

It is important when knitting with more than one color to keep your gauge correct, as it easy to pull the loops of yarn too tight, puckering the work. If you tend to knit colorwork too tightly, increase your needle size for the colorwork section.

Finishing methods

Pressing

Block out each piece of knitting by pinning it on a board to the correct measurements in the pattern. Then lightly press it according to the ball band instructions, omitting any ribbed areas. Take special care to press the edges, as this makes sewing up easier and neater. If you cannot press the fabric, then cover the knitted fabric with a damp cloth and allow it to stand for a couple of hours.

Darn in all ends neatly along the selvedge edge or a color join, as appropriate.

Stitching seams

When you stitch the pieces together, match any areas of color and texture carefully where they meet. Use a special seam stitch, called mattress stitch, as it creates the flattest seam. When complete, press the seams and hems. Lastly, sew on the buttons to correspond with the positions of the buttonholes.

Abbreviations

alt	alternate
approx	approximately
beg	begin(s)(ning)
cm	centimeters
cont	continu(e)(ing)
dec	decreas(e)(ing)
DPN	double-pointed needle
foll	follow(s)(ing)
g	gram
in	inch(es)
inc	increas(e)(ing)
k	knit
k2tog	knit next 2 stitches together
m1	make one stitch by picking up horizontal loop before next stitch and knitting into back of it
m	meters
p	purl
patt	pattern
psso	pass slipped stitch over
p2tog	purl next 2 stitches together
p3tog	purl next 3 stitches together
rem	remain(s)(ing)
rep	repeat
rev St st	reverse stockinette stitch
RS	right side
s2kpo	slip 2 stitches tog, knit 1, pass slipped sts over
skpo	slip 1, k1, psso
sk2po	slip 1, k2tog, psso
sl 1	slip one stitch
sl2tog	slip 2 stitches together
st(s)	stitch(es)
St st	stockinette stitch (1 row knit, 1 row purl)
tbl	through back of loop(s)
tog	together
WS	wrong side
yd	yard(s)
yo	yarn over
yrn	yarn round needle
y2rn	yarn wrapped twice round needle
[ ]/*	repeat instructions within square brackets or between asterisks

yarn information

Rowan yarns

The yarns used in this book are all Rowan yarns. Their specifications are given here. If you use a substitute yarn, take care to match the required gauge by doing a test swatch of the chosen substitution and changing needle size as necessary.

Cotton Glacé

A 100 percent cotton yarn; 1¾oz (125yd/115m) per ball. Recommended gauge: 23 sts and 32 rows to 4in/10cm in St st using size 3–5 (3.25-3.75mm) knitting needles.

Felted Tweed DK

A wool-alpaca-viscose mix (50 percent merino wool, 25 percent alpaca wool, 25 percent viscose); 1¾oz (approx 191yd/175m) per ball. Recommended gauge: 22–24 sts and 30–32 rows to 4in/10cm in St st using size 5–6 (3.5–4mm) knitting needles.

Rowan Fine Tweed

A 100 percent pure wool; 1oz (approx 90yd/98m) per ball. Recommended gauge: 26½ sts and 38 rows to 4in/10cm in St st using size 3 (3.25mm) knitting needles.

Siena 4 Ply

A 100 percent mercerized cotton yarn; 1¾oz (153yd/140m) per ball. Recommended gauge: 28 sts and 38 rows to 4in/10cm in St st using size 2/3 (2.75-3mm) knitting needles.

Wool Cotton

A wool/cotton blend yarn (50 percent merino wool/50 percent cotton); 1¾oz (123yd/113m) per ball. Recommended gauge: 22-24sts and 30-32 rows to 4in/10cm in St st using size 5-6 (3.75-4mm) knitting needles.

Wool Cotton 4 Ply

A wool/cotton blend yarn (50 percent merino wool/50 percent cotton); 1¾oz (197yd/180m) per ball. Recommended gauge: 28 sts and 36 rows to 4in/10cm in St st using size 2 (3.25mm) knitting needles.

resources

U.S.A.
Westminster Fibers Inc,
Nashua, NH 03060
Tel: (800) 445-9276
www.westminsterfibers.com

U.K.
Rowan, Green Lane Mill, Holmfirth,
West Yorkshire, HD9 2DX
Tel: +44 (0) 1484 681881
www.knitrowan.com

AUSTRALIA
Australian Country Spinners Pty Ltd,
Melbourne 3004
Tel: 03 9380 3830
Email: tkohut@auspinners.com.au

BENELUX
Coats Benelux, Ninove, 9400
Tel: 00 32 54 318989
Email: sales.coatsninove@coats.com

CANADA
See U.S.A.

CHINA
Coats Shanghai Ltd, Shanghai
Tel: 86 21 5774 3733
Email: victor.li@coats.com

DENMARK
Coats HP A/S, Copenhagen
Tel: 45 35 86 90 49
www.coatscrafts.dk

FINLAND
Coats Opti Crafts Oy, Kerava, 04220
Tel: (358) 9 274871
wwwcoatscrafts.fi

FRANCE
Coats Steiner, Mehun-Sur-Yèvre,
18500
Tel: 02 48 23 12 30
www.coatscrafts.fr

GERMANY
Coats GmbH, Kenzingen, 79341
Tel: 07162-14346
www.coatsgmbh.de

HONG KONG
See China

ICELAND
Rowan At Storkurinn, Reykjavik, 101
Tel: 551 8258
www.storkurinn.is

ISRAEL
Beit Hasidkit, Kfar Sava, 44256
Tel: (972) 9 7482381

ITALY
Coats Cucirini srl, Milano, 20126
Tel: (02) 636151
www.coatscucirini.com

KOREA
Coats Korea Co. Lt, Seoul, 137-060
Tel: 82-2-521-6262
www.coatskorea.co.kr

NEW ZEALAND
ACS New Zealand, Christchurch
Tel: 64-3-323-6665

NORWAY
Coats Knappehuset AS, Bergen, 5873
Tel: 55 53 93 00

PORTUGAL
Coats & Clark, Vila Nova de Gaia
4431-968
Tel: 223770700
www.crafts.com.pt

SINGAPORE
Golden Dragon Store, Singapore
Tel: (65) 65358454/65358234
Email: gdscraft@hotmail.com

SOUTH AFRICA
Arthur Bales Ltd, Johannesburg, 2195
Tel: (27) 118 882 401
www.arthurbales.co.za

SPAIN
Coats Fabra, Barcelona, 08030
Tel: (34) 93 290 84 00
www.coatscrafts.es

SWEDEN
Coats Expotex AB, Goteborg, 431 30
Tel: (46) 33 720 79 00
www.coatscrafts.se

SWITZERLAND
Coats Stroppel AG, Turgi (AG), CH-5300
Tel: 056 298 12 20
www.coatscrafts.ch

TAIWAN
Cactus Quality Co Ltd, Taiwan, R.O.C.
10084
Tel: 00886-2-23656527
www.excelcraft.com.tw

For stockists in all other countries
please contact Rowan for details

acknowledgments

Author's acknowledgments

A huge thank you to the following team of people, without whose skills this book would not have been possible: Steven and Susan for their brilliant work on photography, art direction, and styling (and to our lovely gang of models); Anne, for her gorgeous page layouts; our fabulous pattern writer, Penny, and her team of fantastic knitters; plus Katie and Marilyn, for their careful editing and checking; Frances for the beautifully knitted swatches; and the entire Rowan team for their continued support.

Finally, special thanks to my partner, Mark, and Billy and Bunny (our adored cats!), and my loving family.

Publisher's acknowledgments

The publishers would like to thank the following individuals for their valuable contribution to this book: Steven Wooster for photography; Anne Wilson for design; Katie Hardwicke for editing; Ed Berry for illustrations; Therese Chynoweth for charts; Penny Hill and her team for pattern writing and knitting; and Marilyn Wilson for pattern checking. Particular thanks to the parents of the babies and children who modeled the knitwear with both brio and aplomb: Albert, Arlo, Jackson, Junia, Lexi, Martha, Noa (who amused herself and us by creating the scarecrow artwork from surplus props on page 78), and Zena. Special thanks, too, to Harriet Carver, India Cummins, Sarah Sinclair, Sarah Tolner, and Catherine Tough for allowing us to use their homes as locations (and thanks to Jem Weston for starting the ball rolling on the model hunt).